¡Viva el español!

Student Edition

¿Qué tal?

John De Mado

Linda West Tibensky

Marcela Gerber, Series Consultant

Mc
Graw
Hill
Education

MHEonline.com

Send all inquiries to:
McGraw-Hill Education
8787 Orion Place
Columbus, OH 43240

ISBN: 978-0-07-602916-7
MHID: 0-07-602916-6

Printed in the United States of America.

13 14 15 16 17 18 QVS 19 18 17 16 15

Contenido

Unidad 3

Unidad 4

Unidad 5

Unidad 6

Unidad 7

Unidad 8

Unidad 9

Unidad 10

Unidad 11

Unidad 12

¡Viva el español!

Student Edition

¿Qué tal?

Un nuevo año

Objetivos

- To review what you have already learned in *¡Hola!*

- To greet your friends in Spanish, ask how they are, and respond as appropriate

- To use numbers for math, counting, telling time, and giving dates

- To identify and describe objects in Spanish

- To talk about the weather and seasons

Courtyard of a school in Bilbao, Spain

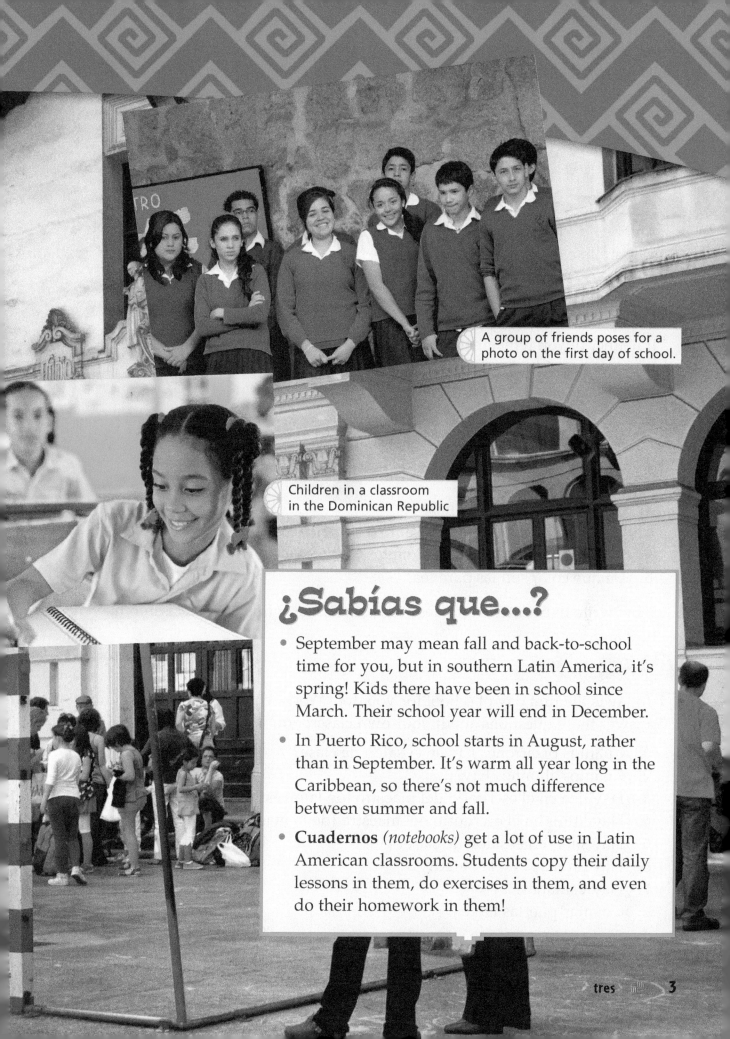

A group of friends poses for a photo on the first day of school.

Children in a classroom in the Dominican Republic

¿Sabías que...?

- September may mean fall and back-to-school time for you, but in southern Latin America, it's spring! Kids there have been in school since March. Their school year will end in December.

- In Puerto Rico, school starts in August, rather than in September. It's warm all year long in the Caribbean, so there's not much difference between summer and fall.

- **Cuadernos** (*notebooks*) get a lot of use in Latin American classrooms. Students copy their daily lessons in them, do exercises in them, and even do their homework in them!

¡Úsalo!

A Here's a look at a classroom in Latin America. Today is the first day of school. Take turns with a partner asking and answering these questions. If you don't remember one of the words, ask your partner. If neither of you remembers, ask your teacher or look it up in the Word List at the end of the book.

1. ¿Cuántos pizarrones hay?
   ¿De qué color es / son?
2. ¿Cuántos alumnos hay en la clase?
3. ¿Quién habla a los alumnos?
4. ¿Cómo es la clase? ¿Es interesante o aburrida?
5. ¿Hay pupitres en la clase? ¿Cuántos?
6. ¿De qué color son las paredes?

Now write five sentences to describe some other things in the classroom.

B Today is the first day of school for you, too! Work with a partner to ask and answer these questions about your own classroom.

1. ¿Cuántos pizarrones hay en el salón de clase?
2. ¿Cuántos alumnos hay?
3. ¿Hay tiza en el escritorio del maestro (de la maestra)?
4. ¿Hay libros en el escritorio del maestro (de la maestra)?
5. ¿Hay sillas en el salón de clase?
6. ¿Hay un mapa en la pared?
7. ¿Hay ventanas?
8. ¿Cuántas puertas hay?

C You're visiting a museum that has some unusual pictures of animals. Take turns with a partner asking and answering questions about the pictures.

> **MODELO** —¿Qué hay en el cuadrado?
>
> —En el cuadrado hay cuatro ratones.

1. ¿Cuántos loros hay?
2. ¿Hay cinco canarios en el triángulo?
3. ¿De qué color son los flamencos?
4. ¿Es rojo el loro?
5. ¿Qué son los animales amarillos?
6. ¿Qué hay en el círculo?
7. ¿Son blancos los ratones?
8. ¿Cuántos animales hay?

D Make a chart like the one below. Look at the shapes and put each one into the correct column. Take turns with your partner making up sentences about them.

> **MODELO** El círculo rojo es pequeño.

pequeño	grande	largo	corto
el círculo rojo			

E Your big brother is in high school. You're talking about what he does during the week, according to the schedule below.

Partner A: Ask your brother questions about what he does during the week.

Partner B: You're the big brother. Answer the questions according to your schedule.

> **MODELO** —¿Vas a la biblioteca el lunes?
>
> —Sí, voy a la biblioteca el lunes.
>
> —¿Vas al parque el jueves?
>
> —No. No voy al parque el jueves.

lunes	martes	miércoles	jueves	viernes	sábado	domingo
la biblioteca	la clase de música	la clase de ciencias	la clase de español	la clase de arte	el cine	el parque
la tienda		el gimnasio	la clase de computadoras		el gimnasio	

F Get together with a partner. Take turns asking and telling your partner when these classes take place. Answer truthfully. If the day of the week for these classes varies, answer for this week.

> **MODELO** —¿Cuándo hay clase de música?
>
> —Hay clase de música los jueves. *or* Hay clase de música el jueves. *or* No hay clase de música.

la clase de música	la clase de ciencias	la clase de matemáticas
la clase de español	la clase de computadoras	la clase de arte
la clase de educación física		

 Think of what you do in each of these classes or places listed below. Write what you do on cards. Show your cards to a partner, who will ask you questions based on the cards. Then switch roles.

Partner A: Ask a question according to the card.

Partner B: Answer the question truthfully.

> estudiar los animales

MODELO —¿En qué clase estudias los animales?

—Estudio los animales en la clase de ciencias.

la clase de música	la clase de estudios sociales	el gimnasio
la clase de computadoras	la clase de arte	la biblioteca

CONEXIÓN CON LOS ESTUDIOS SOCIALES

Maps Draw a map of your school. Include all the places you know in Spanish and label them. Draw four to six classmates in different rooms. Then get together with a partner—but don't show each other your maps!

Your partner asks you questions about your map to figure out whom you drew and where you put them. He or she takes notes and writes sentences about who and where they are. Then switch roles. When you finish, compare your notes to the actual maps. You and your partner can use questions like these:

MODELO ¿Cuántos alumnos hay?

¿Quiénes son?

¿Hay un(a) alumno(a) en... ?

H This is the new classroom you're in this year. Get together with a partner. Describe things in the classroom by using these descriptive words. Make sure to use the correct endings. Your partner will guess what you're describing. Then switch roles.

| MODELO | —Son pequeños. |
| | —Los pupitres son pequeños. |

grande	pequeño	largo	corto	alto
bajo	flaco	gordo	rojo	azul
amarillo	blanco	negro	rosado	anaranjado

I Write riddles about things in your own classroom. Your partner has to guess what you're talking about! Use all the descriptive words and shapes you know, and include objects and people.

| MODELO | —La maestra escribe en el rectángulo grande y verde. ¿Qué es? |
| | —¿Es el pizarrón? |

Entre amigos

Play "Alphabet Brainstorm"!

On this page, you see the Spanish alphabet. Get together in a group with three or four classmates. Your group's job is to think of words you've learned that begin with each letter of the alphabet. The trick is that you can't use any books, notes, or dictionaries!

Copy down the Spanish alphabet for your group. Leave enough room around each letter to write a few words.

Your teacher will time you for five minutes. Think of words that begin with each letter and write them near the letter.

The maximum number of words you and your group can write for each letter is five. Each correctly spelled word scores one point for your team.

Some letters are harder than others, and there will be some for which you don't know any words. Do the easier ones first.

Add up your group's points. Which group is the class champion?

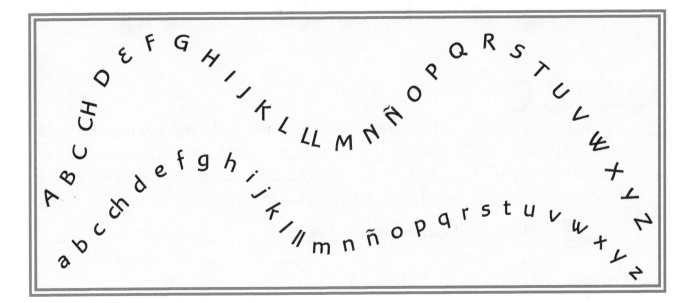

J It's time to change classrooms. Everyone's going to their next class. Answer your partner's questions according to the picture. Take turns asking and answering.

MODELO —¿Quién va a la clase de computadoras?

—Miguel va a la clase de computadoras.

K Stand in a circle with four classmates. Go around the circle and say how many of something there are in the picture above. You can't repeat any items that your classmates have already said! If a person can't think of an item or says the wrong one, he or she has to sit down. The last person standing wins!

MODELO —Hay (doce) estudiantes.

L Look at this list of things you have to do in the afternoon this week. Copy the chart and decide when you will do each activity. Write down specific times. Then ask your partner what he or she will be doing each afternoon this week. Note your partner's answers on the chart. Then switch roles.

MODELO —¿Cuándo vas a patinar y a estudiar inglés?

—El jueves a las cuatro de la tarde.

	yo	mi compañero
patinar y estudiar inglés	el jueves; a las 4	
nadar y estudiar ciencias		
usar la computadora y leer libros		
ir a la biblioteca y cantar		
ir a la casa de Andrés y estudiar matemáticas		
hablar con un amigo y escribir en el cuaderno		
caminar al parque y pintar		

Are both of you doing the same things on some days? Tell the class which activities they are.

MODELO —Vamos a patinar el jueves.

M As you get to know new classmates, you find out that they all have different likes and dislikes. Look at the pairs of items below.

Partner A: For each pair, ask your partner to choose the one he or she likes best.

Partner B: Answer as you like.

> **MODELO** —¿Cuál te gusta, el loro rojo o el loro azul?
>
> —Me gusta el rojo.

1. las clases fáciles / las clases difíciles
2. el flamenco blanco / el flamenco rosado
3. el lápiz corto / el lápiz largo
4. el maestro divertido / el maestro aburrido
5. los cines grandes / los cines pequeños
6. el oso negro / el oso marrón
7. los libros largos / los libros cortos
8. la mariposa gris / la mariposa morada

N You want to know more about your classmates. In groups of three, take turns asking and answering the questions. With whom do you have more things in common? Report to the class three things you found out from the person you have the most in common with.

1. ¿A qué hora vas a la escuela?
2. ¿Cuántas clases tienes?
3. ¿Cuál es tu clase favorita?
4. ¿Cómo es tu clase favorita?
5. ¿Siempre comprendes las matemáticas?
6. ¿Te gusta la clase de estudios sociales?
7. ¿Lees mucho en la biblioteca?

O Get together with a partner and make two sets of cards with the following words.

Set A:

cantar	patinar	caminar	estudiar	pintar
practicar	nadar	bailar	usar	

Set B:

bien	mal	a la escuela	en la escuela
en la clase de arte	deportes	en verano	la computadora

Put the cards facedown in two separate piles. Now, take turns drawing a card from each pile. Form a sentence with the words on the cards. For example, if you draw **patinar** and **en la clase de arte,** you can say: **Patino en la clase de arte.** Your partner has to say whether this is possible or not. **(Es posible. / No es posible.)** You get to keep the cards that make sense together. The player with the most cards at the end wins!

CONEXIÓN CON LAS MATEMÁTICAS

Telling Time Look at these clocks. Take turns with a partner telling the time.

MODELO —**Son las diez menos cuarto de la mañana.**

CONEXIÓN CON LAS CIENCIAS

Weather and Seasons A group of students from Uruguay is visiting your school. They have a lot of questions about the local weather and seasons.

Your teacher will assign you a month to tell them about. With a partner, write at least five sentences describing the month and add a drawing or collage showing the season for that month. Here are some words and expressions you could use.

Las estaciones

el invierno	la primavera	el verano	el otoño

Los meses

enero	febrero	marzo	abril	mayo	junio
julio	agosto	septiembre	octubre	noviembre	diciembre

El tiempo

Hace sol.	Hace calor.	Hace frío.	Hace fresco.	Hace viento.
Está nublado.	Nieva.	Llueve.	Hace buen tiempo.	

Otras expresiones

siempre	nunca	a veces
mucho	poco *(a little)*	Hace (cuarenta) grados.

And here's an example of what you might say:

Enero es un mes de invierno. Hace mucho frío y a veces nieva. A veces está nublado. A veces llueve. Nunca hace calor, pero a veces hace sol.

Your teacher will name months of the year. If you wrote about one of the months your teacher names, volunteer to read your description to the class.

P Get together with a partner. Act out one of these expressions while your partner tries to guess how you feel. When your partner guesses correctly, switch roles. Continue until you have used all the expressions.

MODELO —¿Tienes hambre?

—No, no tengo hambre. *or* Sí, tengo hambre.

(Tener)	calor	miedo	frío	hambre	la gripe
	sed	sueño	razón	prisa	suerte

Q Look at these pictures. Secretly choose one and write down its number. Your partner asks you questions to guess which picture you picked. Then switch roles.

MODELO —¿Cuántos lápices tienes?

—Tengo tres lápices.

1.
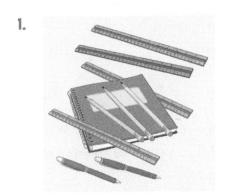

2.

3.

4.
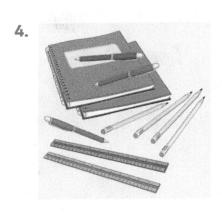

5.

6.

Unidad de repaso

Your teacher will ask students in the class to put an item of theirs on the teacher's desk. Your teacher will look away while students go to the front of the room and place their items on the desk.

Then your teacher will hold up each item and ask who it belongs to. Feel free to jump in if you know whose it is!

MODELO —¿De quién es el bolígrafo azul?

—Es mi bolígrafo azul. *or* Es el bolígrafo azul de Elena.

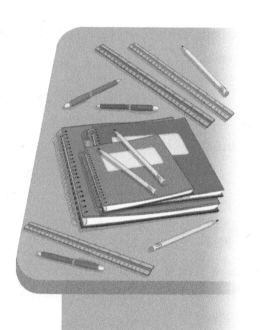

R You want to find out what your partner is doing next weekend. If you like what your partner is doing, say that you're also going to do it. Do you like the same things?

MODELO —¿Qué vas a hacer el próximo fin de semana?

—Voy a patinar.

—¡Yo también! *or* Yo no.

S What time of day is it in each picture? Is it morning, noon, afternoon, or night? Write the time of day and discuss it with your partner. Point to things in the picture that make you think it's that time of day.

1.

2.

3.

4.

 CONEXIÓN CON LAS MATEMÁTICAS

Adding and Subtracting Dates

Tell your partner about your family and about when they were born. Your partner will use addition and subtraction to tell you their ages. Use actual birthdates or make them up if you're not sure. You can tell your partner the birth year in English, and your partner will then give the age in Spanish. Switch roles after telling your partner four dates.

> **MODELO** —Mi tío Carlos / 7 de mayo de 1967
>
> —Tu tío Carlos tiene (treinta y siete) años.

Get in a group with two or three classmates. Write a set of cards with these words on them (one phrase on each card):

Now write a second set of cards with these words:

Put the two sets of cards into two piles. Draw a card from pile 1—for example, **la hermana.** Show it to the group.

Then draw a card from pile 2—for example, **mi mamá.** Now put the two words into a sentence stating their relationship:

La hermana de mi mamá es...

Does your group know the answer? It's **mi tía.** Return the two cards to the bottom of the piles, and then it's the next classmate's turn. What combinations are you going to come up with?

T **¡Pobre Esteban!** *(Poor Esteban!)* He wrote some paragraphs for school, but lost them. Help him rewrite his homework. Take turns reading his notes to a partner, and help your partner choose the best phrase to complete the last sentence.

> **MODELO** **Sarita tiene clase de matemáticas a las dos. No le gusta la clase y siempre tiene sueño. La clase...**
>
>   **a.** es muy interesante.
>
>   **b.** es muy divertida.
>
>   **c.** **es muy aburrida.**

1. El Sr. Silva tiene una casa grande. Siempre hay muchas personas en su casa: su bisabuelo, sus papás, su hermano, sus cuatro hijas y sus cinco hijos. El señor Silva...
   a. tiene un gimnasio en la casa.
   b. tiene una familia pequeña.
   c. tiene una familia grande.

2. Berta tiene suerte. Va a ir a la casa de su amiga Amalia. A Berta le gustan mucho los animales, y a Amalia también. Amalia...
   a. tiene cuarenta cuadernos rosados.
   b. tiene dos hermanas y un hermano.
   c. tiene tres gatos, siete loros y diez peces.

3. Simón no tiene hambre. A veces tiene frío. También tiene sueño. ¡Pobre Simón! Él...
   a. tiene la gripe.
   b. tiene miedo.
   c. tiene suerte.

4. La mamá de Alberto tiene una hermana, Sofía. Sofía tiene una hija que se llama Susana. Susana es...
   a. la nieta de Sofía.
   b. la prima de Alberto.
   c. la hermana de Alberto.

U Ask your partner if he or she likes the things on this list. Copy the chart and keep track of the answers.

> **MODELO** —¿Paula, te gustan las matemáticas?
>
> —No.

	Sí	No
las matemáticas		✓
ir al gimnasio		
las ciencias		
las computadoras		
el fútbol		

Then switch partners. Your new partner will ask you questions about your first partner's likes and dislikes. After you answer, your new partner reacts to what you say.

> **MODELO** —¿A Paula le gustan las matemáticas?
>
> —No, no le gustan.
>
> —A mí tampoco. *or* A mí me gustan.

V Look at this picture with a partner and decide together who might be whom (**el abuelo, la nieta, el papá,** etc.). Write as many words as you can that apply to each person. For example, **la nieta** can also be someone else's **prima.** Write descriptions of each person.

> **MODELO** —Es el abuelo de ella.
>
> El abuelo es alto.

Entre amigos

With this sentence code grid, you can make up sentences, even wild and crazy ones!

Use the letters across the top and the numbers down the side to identify a square. For example, square A1 contains the word **yo.** Combine that with squares D1 and C6, and you get A1—D1—C6, or **Yo leo un libro.**

	A	B	C	D	E
1	yo	muy bien	nunca	leer	mucho
2	aprender	muy interesante	escribir	la tienda	Sr./Sra./Srta. *(your teacher's name)*
3	ella	él	la casa de mi amigo	no	simpático
4	mi perro	en	ser	terrible	a veces
5	la escuela	tú	un cuaderno	usted	estudiar
6	la clase de español	ir (a)	un libro	el cine	muy divertido

Write code sentences, then get together with two or three classmates to see if they can figure them out. Include all the parts you need, and don't forget that some words will change form when you use them in sentences. It's fun, and at the same time, ¡B5—A2—E1!

1

Las partes del cuerpo

Objetivos

- To name parts of your body
- To name parts of your head and face
- To tell people what hurts you
- To ask people if something hurts them

Hikers walk over hardened lava flow on Volcán Arenal in Costa Rica.

A woman sells natural remedies in La Paz, Bolivia.

A group of Spanish children play soccer at school.

¿Sabías que...?

- In some places in the Spanish-speaking world, adults may pull your ear on your birthday, one pull for every year.

- If a Spanish-speaking person taps on his or her elbow when talking about someone, it means the person he or she is talking about doesn't like to spend money.

- In Spanish, you can say the word **¡Ojo!** *(eye)* to mean "Be careful!" or "Watch out!"

¿Cómo se dice?

¿Cuáles son las partes del cuerpo?

—El brazo es una parte del cuerpo.

—Sí. Correcto.

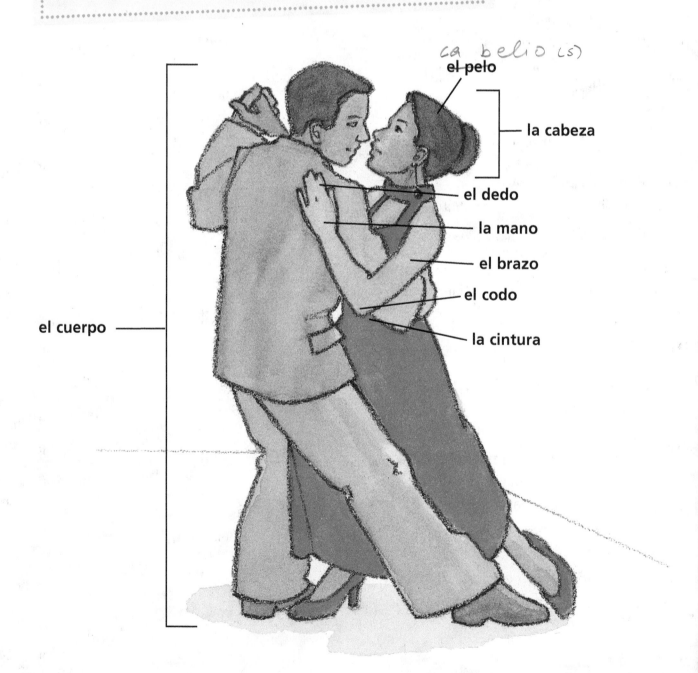

ca belio (s)
el pelo

la cabeza

el dedo

la mano

el brazo

el codo

la cintura

el cuerpo

—¿Vas a bailar?

—No, no voy a bailar.

—¿Por qué no?

—Porque me duele el tobillo.

el cuello

el hombro

la espalda

la rodilla

la pierna

el tobillo

el pie

CONEXIÓN CON LA CULTURA

Tango is a typical dance that started in the city of Buenos Aires, Argentina. It first appeared more than a hundred years ago, but now it's enjoyed by people in many parts of the world! It is danced in places as far away from Argentina as France and Japan, and by people of all ages. What are the names of some of the dances you know?

¡Úsalo!

Get together with two classmates. Draw a paper doll. Write all the names of the different parts of the body on cards. Take turns picking cards and placing each of them on the correct part of the body that you drew. Point to the part of the body and say what it is.

MODELO —Es el hombro.

Entre amigos

Play a game with four or five classmates. Take turns being the leader. The leader gets five turns asking the rest of the group to say which part of his or her own body he or she is touching.

The leader asks **¿Qué toco?,** as he or she touches a part of the body—for example, his or her hand. The first person to answer correctly **(la mano)** gets a point.

See how fast you can play the game! The student with the highest number of points after two rounds wins.

CONEXIÓN CON LAS MATEMÁTICAS

Measurements It's time to take some measurements! Get together with four or five classmates. Help each other take the following measurements in centimeters:

1. the circumference of your head

2. your arm, from your shoulder to your wrist

3. your leg, from your knee to your ankle

As a group, fill out a chart like this one with everyone's measurements.

	Juan	Ana	Pedro	Isabel	Marcos
cabeza					
brazo					
pierna					

Then find the median, the mode, and the range of your measurements. Make sure you say these numbers in Spanish!

En resumen

¿Cuáles son las partes del cuerpo?

el brazo	la cabeza
el codo	la cintura
el cuello	la espalda
el dedo	la mano
el hombro	la pierna
el pelo	la rodilla
el pie	
el tobillo	

¿Cómo se dice?

¿Qué parte de la cara es?

—¿Qué parte de la cara es?

—Es la frente, por supuesto.

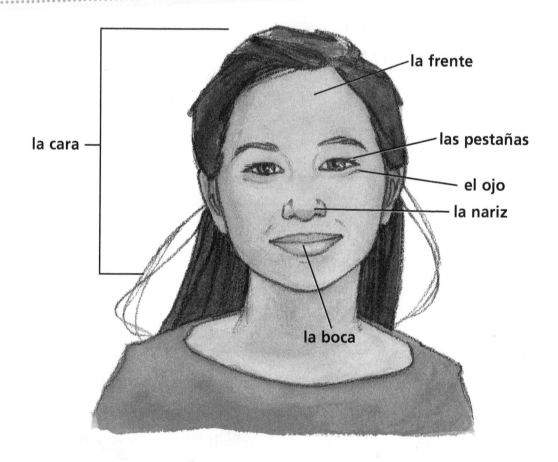

la frente

las pestañas

el ojo

la nariz

la cara

la boca

¿Sabías que...?

Ouch! Is that what you say when you hurt yourself? If a Spanish-speaking person gets hurt— for example, stubs a toe or closes a door on a finger—he or she is likely to say **¡Ay!**

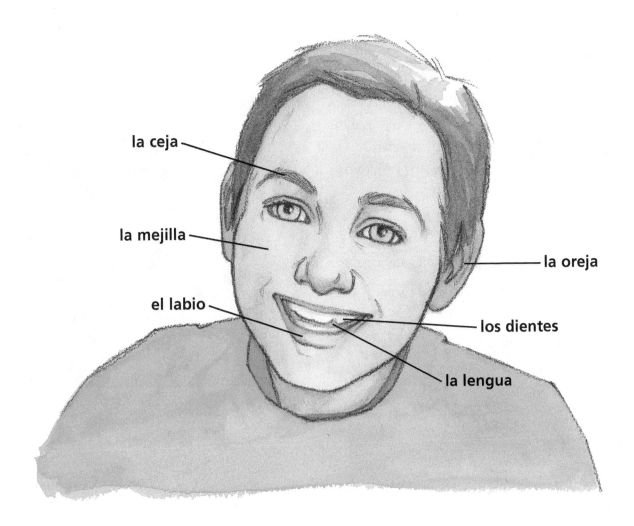

la ceja

la mejilla

el labio

la oreja

los dientes

la lengua

 ## CONEXIÓN CON LA CULTURA

Idioms In English, if something is very expensive you can say, "It costs an arm and a leg." In Spanish, you'd say **Cuesta un ojo de la cara.** Spanish has many other expressions that talk about parts of the body. Here's another one:

Tiene los ojos más grandes que la boca.
His eyes are bigger than his stomach.

What are the differences between the two versions?

¡Úsalo!

A Look at the face in the photo. Have you seen something like this before? This is an Olmec face. Talk about it with a partner. Use the questions to help you describe it.

1. ¿Cómo es la nariz?

2. ¿Son grandes o pequeñas las orejas?

3. ¿Son grandes o pequeños los labios?

4. ¿Tiene cejas?

5. ¿Es grande la cara?

6. ¿Cuántos ojos tiene la cara?

B Fill out a chart like this one with a partner. Take turns asking each other the questions.

¿Qué parte o partes del cuerpo usas para...	
comer una pizza?	
leer un libro?	
cantar?	
escuchar?	
caminar por el parque?	
bailar?	
jugar al fútbol?	
usar la computadora?	
nadar?	

CONEXIÓN CON EL ARTE

Symmetry Look at these paintings. Decide which faces are symmetrical, that is, have balanced facial features.

Compara

En inglés	En español
symmetry	la simetría
symmetrical	simétrico(a)

En resumen

¿Qué parte de la cara **es**?

Es el labio.   **Son** los dientes.
el ojo.   las pestañas.

la boca.
la ceja.
la frente.
la lengua.
la mejilla.
la nariz.
la oreja.

¿Cómo se dice?

Talking about what hurts

Look at these pictures and sentences. They show you how to talk about things that hurt you and others.

Me duele la cabeza.

¿Te duele la cabeza?

¿Le duele la cabeza?

Me duelen los pies.

¿Te duelen los pies?

Le duelen los pies.

To talk about what hurts, you use the verb **doler.** When you want to say that something hurts you, use **me duele.** If more than one thing hurts, such as both of your feet, use **me duelen.** Notice that **doler** works just like the verb **gustar.**

When you're asking someone if something hurts him or her, use **te duele.** If you think more than one thing is hurting the person, use **te duelen.**

When you're talking about someone else, use **le duele** or **le duelen.**

¿Sabías que...?

In English, you say that a part of the body is yours: *My* tooth hurts. But Spanish speakers don't use the possessive form ("my") when they talk about their body. They use "the" (**el, la, los** or **las**) instead: **Me duelen los dientes.** Notice that the word **Me** already lets you know whose teeth you're talking about.

¡Úsalo!

A Your little sister has fallen off her bicycle. You're trying to find out what hurts her. Use the pictures to complete your questions. Your partner will answer.

> **MODELO** —¿Te duelen los hombros?
>
> —Sí, me duelen los hombros.
> *or* No, no me duelen los hombros.

1.  2.  3.  4.

B Rodrigo is in bad shape. Look at the pictures and tell a partner what you think hurts. Then switch roles.

> **MODELO** —Le duele la cabeza.

1. 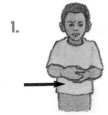 2.  3.  4.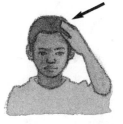

C Play a game of "Hot and Cold"! Get together with a partner and think of a part of the body. Imagine that it hurts. Then your partner asks you if something hurts. Say **frío** if the part of the body is *far* from the one you wrote down. Say **caliente** ("hot") if your partner is getting close! Switch roles after each correct guess.

> **MODELO** —¿Te duelen los pies?
>
> —No me duelen los pies. Frío.

D Some of your friends aren't well. They can't do the things that they normally do. Read the sentences to a partner. Your partner figures out what part of the body might be hurting. Take turns asking and answering.

Partner A: Read the sentence.

Partner B: Say a part of the body that hurts, according to the activity.

MODELO —Adriana no camina.

—Le duele el tobillo. *or* Le duelen los pies.

1. Javier no habla.
2. Rosa no usa la computadora.
3. Alicia no escribe.
4. Ramón no lee.
5. Francisco no practica deportes.
6. Blanca no baila.

 ## CONEXIÓN CON LAS CIENCIAS

Pain Why do you feel pain? Pain is a very important protective device that your nervous system uses to let you know you should stop doing something. When a part of the body begins to hurt, nerve endings in that part of the body pick up the stimuli and send electrical signals to the brain. These signals tell the brain that the body is doing something that is not good for it, and you feel pain.

Here are the five senses. In Spanish, tell your partner the body part(s) related to each sense. Then, using one of your favorite tunes, write five lines to a song to help you remember the five senses.

el tacto (*touch*)
el gusto (*taste*)
el olfato (*smell*)

la vista (*sight*)
el oído (*hearing*)

Entre amigos

Sit in a circle with six or seven classmates. Face outward, so you can't see each other.

Choose two group members to stand inside the circle. One is a "bellyacher," who silently acts out the pain. The other is a "caretaker," who makes sure that the students guessing don't peek and that the bellyacher doesn't change the type of pain.

Each group member gets two chances to guess what the bellyacher's pain is. They ask the caretaker questions such as: **¿Le duele el codo?** or **¿Le duelen los pies?**

If group members can't guess the pain, they end the round by asking the bellyacher: **¿Qué te duele?** The bellyacher answers, and the others can turn around and look. Continue the game by naming new caretakers and bellyachers.

¿Sabías que...?

In many Spanish-speaking countries, you can find a pharmacy by looking for a green cross. What symbols identify pharmacies where you live?

En resumen

¿Qué te duele?

Me duele		Me duelen	
Te duele	la cabeza.	**Te duelen**	las piernas.
Le duele		**Le duelen**	

¿Cómo se dice?

Talking about what hurts a specific person

You already know how to talk about what hurts you, someone you're talking to, or another person.

But what if you want to say exactly who it is you're talking about? Look at these sentences:

A Carlos le duelen los dedos.

A la señora le duele la espalda.

A similar thing happens when you're talking to an adult. You would use the word **usted,** like this:

Señor, ¿**a usted** le duele la cabeza?

Notice that you must use the word **a** before a person's name or the words that identify him or her, including **usted.** This happens with both **gustar** and **doler.**

Remember that Spanish speakers often don't say the name of the person. They only say it when they want to make it especially clear or to avoid confusion.

CONEXIÓN CON LA SALUD

Back Health Do you know how to take care of your back? Heavy backpacks (**mochilas**) can be bad for you! Follow these tips to avoid hurting your back:

- Your backpack should not weigh more than $\frac{1}{10}$ of your own weight.
- It's better to have a small backpack: the bigger it is, the more stuff you will want to put in it!
- If the backpack has different sections, you can distribute the weight better.
- Put on both straps, one on each shoulder.
- Well-padded and wide adjustable straps are much better for you!

Do a survey of the backpacks in your class to find out who's following these tips and who's not! Ask your classmates: **¿Te duele la espalda?** to find out if heavy backpacks are a problem in your class. Make a pie chart to show what percentage of your class has a problem with heavy backpacks.

¡Úsalo!

A Get together with a partner and make two sets of cards. On one set, write the names that are in Column A. On the other set, write the parts of the body that are in Column B.

Put each set facedown in a pile. Take turns with your partner picking a card from each pile. Form a sentence with the cards to say which part of the body hurts that person. If you say it correctly, you get to keep the cards. The one with more cards at the end wins!

MODELO —A Antonio le duelen las piernas.

Column A	Column B
Antonio	las piernas
Lola	la frente
Pedro	los ojos
Silvia	las orejas
Berta	el codo
Manuel	el cuello
Pancho	las manos
Sarita	la rodilla
Paula	los dedos

B Draw a part of the body you know in Spanish on a card. Then get together with five or six classmates and mix your cards. Decide who will be the nurse and who will be the doctor. The rest of you will be patients!

The doctor steps away from the group so that he or she can't hear what the others say. Each patient picks a card. The nurse asks the patients what hurts them according to their cards, and writes their answers on his or her "chart" (a sheet of paper) next to their names.

Then the doctor comes back, and the nurse has to explain what hurts each person.

MODELO —A Marta le duele la cabeza.

Take turns playing the roles.

◎ ◎ ◎ **Compara** ◎ ◎ ◎	
En inglés	**En español**
doctor	el doctor
patient	el paciente

¿Sabías que...?

An *interpreter* is someone who helps people understand each other when they don't speak the same language. For example, a Spanish interpreter who speaks English and Spanish can help patients in the United States who don't speak English so that they can understand their doctor. The doctor asks questions in English and the interpreter repeats them in Spanish to the patient. When the patient answers in Spanish, the interpreter repeats the answers in English to the doctor. Is this something you think you could do one day? Find out if there are professional interpreters in your city.

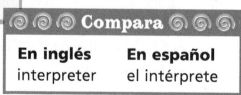

◎ ◎ ◎ **Compara** ◎ ◎ ◎	
En inglés	**En español**
interpreter	el intérprete

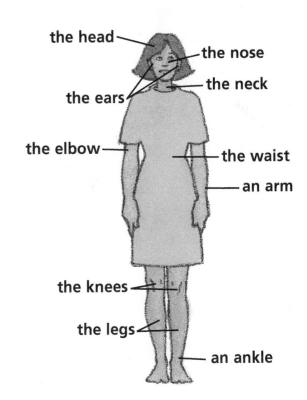

the head
the nose
the neck
the ears
the elbow
the waist
an arm
the knees
the legs
an ankle

C Get together with a partner. Imagine that you're an interpreter at the hospital. You need to ask a patient, who speaks only Spanish, what hurts. Your partner plays the patient and picks a part of the body from this diagram without telling you what it is. You ask if each of the parts of the body listed hurts. Your partner will answer your questions. Remember to use **usted.**

MODELO —¿A usted le duelen las piernas?

Entre amigos

Your teacher will hand out cards with different parts of the body on them. You have to find out who received each one! Go around the classroom asking your classmates questions such as **¿Te duelen los dientes?** They answer **sí** or **no** according to what is pictured on their card.

Write down what each person answers. Then write a report like this one for the whole class.

A _____ le duelen los pies.
A _____ le duele la cabeza.

En resumen

A él	le duele	la cabeza.
A ella	le duelen	las rodillas.
A usted		

| **A** la señora | le duele | la espalda. |
| **A** Carlos | le duelen | los dedos. |

¿Dónde se habla español?

ESPAÑA
Madrid

España

Two traditional forms of entertainment in the culture of Spain are bullfighting and flamenco dancing. Although these are not as popular today as they were years ago, these two traditions represent some of the history, excitement, and color of Spain.

Datos

Capital: Madrid

Ciudades importantes: Barcelona, Bilbao, Sevilla, Valencia

Idiomas oficiales: Español, catalán, vasco, gallego, valenciano

Moneda: El euro

Población: 40.2 millones

¡Léelo en español!

La corrida de toros La corrida de toros viene del tiempo de los romanos en España. Es una costumbre[1] muy antigua. La corrida empieza con un desfile[2] de los toreros[3] y sus ayudantes[4]. Los músicos tocan el pasodoble. En el primer acto, el torero estudia el toro. Hace pases con una capa grande y morada. Los pases se llaman verónicas. Después ponen banderillas, que son palos[5] con cintas de colores. Los picadores entran y quitan fuerza al toro. Luego, en el tercer acto, el torero o matador hace pases muy peligrosos. Está muy cerca del toro y usa la muleta con una capa pequeña y roja. Por fin mata al toro. El pueblo come la carne del toro, o se destina a los pobres. Muchas personas piensan que la corrida es cruel. ¿Qué piensas tú?

¡Léelo en español!

El flamenco   El flamenco es un baile que comenzó en el siglo[6] XIX y viene de los gitanos[7]. Los gitanos llegaron a España de Rumania en el siglo XV.

Los gitanos llevan ropa especial y siguen sus tradiciones. En el baile flamenco, cantan sobre sus vidas, sus emociones y sus problemas. Los hombres llevan trajes negros y camisas blancas. Las mujeres generalmente llevan vestidos de muchos colores. Una o dos personas tocan guitarras, una o dos tocan el cajón y las otras personas tocan las palmas. La música es muy emocionante.

[1] custom   [2] parade   [3] bullfighters   [4] helpers
[5] sticks   [6] century   [7] gypsies

¡Comprendo!

Answer in English.
1. What happens in the three parts of a bullfight?
2. What different roles are there in a bullfight? What does each person do?
3. What are your opinions of the bullfight?
4. What do the men and women wear when dancing the flamenco?
5. What musical instruments are used in flamenco music?

¿Qué ropa llevas?

Department store window
display in La Habana, Cuba

Objetivos

- To describe clothes
- To talk about how your clothes look and fit
- To talk about clothes you're going to buy
- To tell to whom things belong
- To read about shopping and traditional clothing
  in Spanish-speaking countries

The crowd at this Seville, Spain festival wears a mixture of traditional and modern clothing.

An Argentinean gaucho wears a poncho during a cattle drive.

¿Sabías que...?

- In Spanish-speaking countries people can shop for their clothes in all sorts of places, from boutiques and department stores to open-air markets.

- Every country in the Spanish-speaking world has traditional clothing, and there are often different kinds in each region. People wear these traditional clothes at festivals and other special celebrations. But most people usually dress just like you and your friends.

- The Spanish language borrowed the word **poncho** from a native South American language. Indigenous South Americans still use these blankets with an opening for the head to keep warm in the chilly Andes mountains.

¿Cómo se dice?

¿Qué llevas?

—¿Qué ropa llevas hoy?

—Llevo un suéter y una falda.

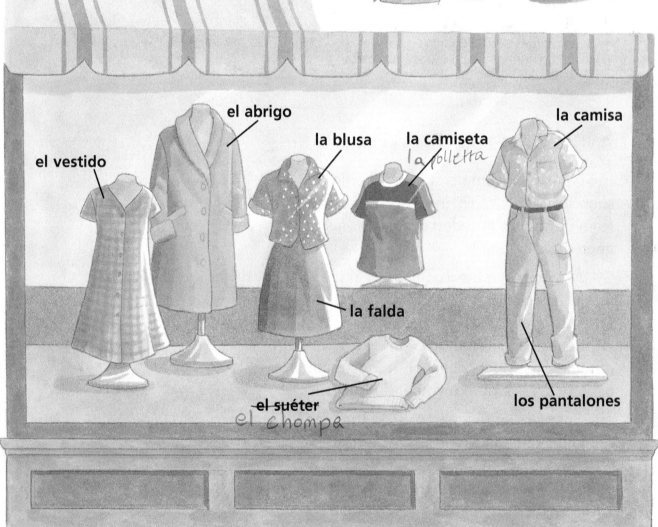

el vestido

el abrigo

la blusa

la camiseta

la polletta

la camisa

la falda

el suéter

el chompa

los pantalones

—¿Qué vas a llevar a la fiesta el sábado?

—Voy a llevar una camiseta y unos pantalones.

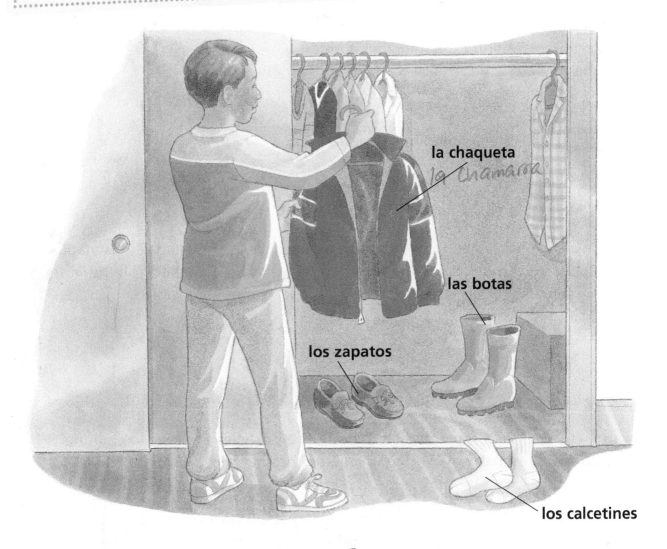

la chaqueta

la chamarra

las botas

los zapatos

los calcetines

 ## CONEXIÓN CON LA CULTURA

Bargaining One of the great things about shopping in markets in Latin America is that the vendors will usually bargain with you. If you ask how much something costs, they'll give you a price higher than they think you'll pay. It's up to you to offer a lower price. Then the fun begins! How well do you think you could bargain?

¡Úsalo!

A Look at this drawing carefully for one minute. Close your book and tell your partner everything that you can remember about the clothes the girl is wearing. Your partner checks your description and adds to it.

> **MODELO** —Lleva una camisa anaranjada, un suéter...

B Sit in a circle with four or five classmates. On a card, draw and color what the person to your right is wearing. Don't write his or her name! Put all the cards in a bag. Then take turns picking out cards and describing the items on them. The first one to say the correct name gets a point!

 ## Entre amigos

Get your parents' permission to bring some articles of their old clothing to school. You can also bring in an older brother's or sister's old clothing as long as it's a couple of sizes too large for you and your classmates.

Put all the clothes into a large pile. One person starts by picking out some items from the pile and putting them on over his or her other clothes. Then that student goes to the front of the class.

Your teacher will choose another student, who has to describe what the first person is wearing.

María lleva unas botas grandes, un vestido largo y una camisa azul.

Keep taking turns until your teacher calls time.

CONEXIÓN CON LAS MATEMÁTICAS

Money Imagine that you received a $100 gift certificate to buy your back-to-school clothes at this store. Decide what you will buy. You can buy anything you want, as long as you stay within the budget! You must buy at least three items.

Make a list of everything you want, and add up the total cost. Try to get the most items for your money! (All prices include tax.)

After you finish your list, get together with a partner and tell him or her what you decided to buy and how much you spent.

MODELO —Voy a comprar un vestido azul...

En resumen

llevar	el abrigo	la blusa
	el suéter	la camisa
	el vestido	la camiseta
	los calcetines	la chaqueta
	los pantalones	la falda
	los zapatos	las botas

¿Cómo se dice?

¿Qué vas a comprar?

Color ⇒ 8ue color

—¿Qué ropa vas a comprar?

—Voy a comprar un traje de baño.

la bata

el sombrero

el impermeable

el pijama

la gorra

las medias

el traje de baño

¿Cómo es?

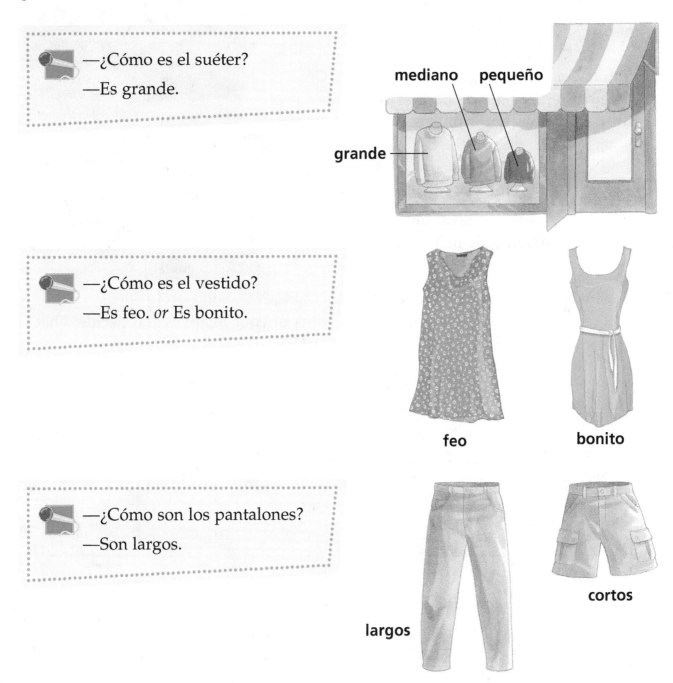

—¿Cómo es el suéter?
—Es grande.

mediano pequeño

grande

—¿Cómo es el vestido?
—Es feo. *or* Es bonito.

feo bonito

—¿Cómo son los pantalones?
—Son largos.

largos cortos

Some words you can use to talk about things are **grande, mediano, mediana, pequeño, pequeña, feo, fea, bonito, bonita, corto, corta, largo,** and **larga.** Remember, **grande** only changes in the plural, when it adds an **-s.** Use **mediano, pequeño, feo, bonito, corto,** and **largo** to describe items that use **el.** Use **mediana, pequeña, fea, bonita, corta,** and **larga** to describe items that use **la.** All of these words add an **-s** in the plural.

¡Úsalo!

A You're going on a trip and need to pack. Get together with a partner. Each of you picks one of the destinations in the photos. Tell your partner what you will wear there.

> **MODELO** —¿Qué vas a llevar?
>
> —Voy a llevar un sombrero, un traje de baño...

B You're going shopping for your family. Think of your relatives and decide what you will buy, and in what size. Make a chart like this one.

	grande	pequeño	mediano	corto	largo

Then get together with a partner and say which items you will buy.

> **MODELO** —Voy a comprar unos pantalones largos y grandes y un impermeable pequeño...

C Get together with a partner. Tell him or her if you like these items of clothing and why.

> **MODELO** —No me gusta el sombrero. Es feo.
>
> —Me gusta. Es bonito.

1.    2.    3.    4.

CONEXIÓN CON LAS CIENCIAS

Temperature Look at the map and tell a partner what people will wear in each city today.

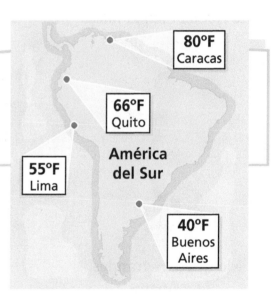

80°F Caracas
66°F Quito
55°F Lima
América del Sur
40°F Buenos Aires

En resumen

Voy a comprar	una bata.	Voy a comprar	un impermeable.
	una gorra.		un pijama.
	unas medias.		un sombrero.
			un traje de baño.

El sombrer**o es**   grand**e**, pequeñ**o**, median**o**, fe**o**, bonit**o**, cort**o**, larg**o**.
La bata **es**   grand**e**, pequeñ**a**, median**a**, fe**a**, bonit**a**, cort**a**, larg**a**.
Los pijamas **son**   grand**es**, pequeñ**os**, median**os**, fe**os**, bonit**os**, cort**os**, larg**os**.
Las medias **son**   grand**es**, pequeñ**as**, median**as**, fe**as**, bonit**as**, cort**as**, larg**as**.

¿Cómo se dice?

Talking about how clothes look

Here's how you talk about how clothes look and fit.

Me **queda** bien la falda.

Te **queda** pequeña
la camisa.

A ella le **queda**
largo el vestido.

Me **quedan** grandes
los zapatos.

Te **quedan** bien
los pantalones.

A él le **quedan** mal
los calcetines.

If something fits you well, use **bien.** If it fits you badly, use **mal.** These words stay the same in all cases.

Use **me** to talk about yourself, **te** to talk to another child or family member, and **le** to talk about someone else or to an adult. Always use **a** before **él, ella,** or the name of a person when you talk about how their clothes fit. However, **él** and **ella** are often skipped in Spanish if everyone knows who you're talking about.

When you're talking about one item of clothing, use **queda.** When you're talking about more than one, use **quedan.**

¡Úsalo!

A Look at these pictures and tell a partner how these clothes fit each person.

> **MODELO** —Le queda bien la falda. Le quedan pequeños los zapatos.

B Play **"Teléfono"** *(Telephone)!* Stand in line with four classmates. Your teacher whispers to the first person how something fits him or her. The first person then whispers to the next one how it fits, according to what the teacher said. In turn, each person whispers to the next person. The last person says out loud what he or she heard.

Partner 1: Tell the next person how something fits the teacher.

Partner 2: Tell the next person how something fits the teacher.

> MODELO —La falda le queda larga.
>
> —La falda le queda larga.

CONEXIÓN CON LA CULTURA

Traditional Clothes Traditional clothes can often tell a lot about the person wearing them. In Guatemala, for example, the designs and patterns on a Guatemalan **huipil,** which is a hand-woven blouse, can tell you the town of the woman wearing it, and sometimes it can even tell you if she is married and has children. The **huipil** is among the most beautiful traditional clothing in the world, with bright colors and unique designs. What do your clothes say about you?

¿Sabías que...?

In some parts of the Andes mountains in Perú, women wear men's small derby hats. They're considered a sign of elegance. How would you describe the way this hat fits the woman?

C Get together with a partner. Draw a doll on a piece of paper. Find pictures of different items of clothing in magazines, and cut them out. Try them on the figure that you drew. Then tell your partner how the clothes fit and what you think of the clothing.

> **MODELO** —Le queda corta la falda. La falda es bonita.

Entre amigos

Be the fashion police! Bring in photos of people dressed in different styles of clothing that you've cut out of a magazine. Then get together with a partner. Take turns asking how a certain item fits and answering the question.

> **MODELO** —¿Cómo le queda el suéter?
>
> —Le queda mal. El suéter es grande y feo.

En resumen

¿Cómo me queda?
Te queda bien.

Me
Te } queda bien / mal.
Le

El vestid**o**	me queda	pequeñ**o**.
La fald**a**		pequeñ**a**.
Los calcetin**es**	me queda**n**	pequeñ**os**.
Las bot**as**		pequeñ**as**.

¿Cómo se dice?

Whose is it?

Study these pictures and sentences. What word is used to show who owns something?

Es el suéter **de** Enrique.

Son los vestidos
de Carmen.

Es el libro **del** alumno.

Son los libros
del maestro.

Es la regla **de** la alumna.

Son las reglas
de la maestra.

In Spanish, you use the word **de** to show ownership of an item or items. If **de** is followed by **el,** the words combine to form the word **del.**

You can also say that something belongs to someone without mentioning the person's name.

Es **de ella.**
Es **de él.**
Es **de usted.**

In English, you'd say "It's hers." or "It's his." or "It's yours."

Now look at these examples to see how to ask to whom an item or items belong. What is different in the three examples?

—**¿De quién es** el libro?
—Es de la alumna.

—**¿De quién son** los bolígrafos?
—Son del alumno.

—**¿De quiénes son** los abrigos?
—Son de los alumnos.

If you think something belongs to *one* person, you ask **¿De quién es... ?**
If you think *several* things belong to *one* person, you ask **¿De quién son... ?**
If you think *several* things belong to *more than one* person, you ask **¿De quiénes son... ?**

¿De quién es el libro?

¡Úsalo!

A Test your memory! Stand in a circle with four classmates. Look carefully at what the others are wearing. Then everyone turns around to face outward. The person on your right asks you a question about what someone in the group is wearing. Think about it before you answer!

> **MODELO** —¿Cómo es la camisa de Tina?
>
> —La camisa de Tina es verde.

Continue playing until everyone gets to ask and answer a question.

B Get together with three or four classmates. Draw an object that you know on one card. Draw several of the same object on another card. Write your name on the back of the cards and shuffle them with your classmates' cards.

Take turns picking a card and showing it. The person to your right asks you whose it is. Look at the name on the card to answer.

> **MODELO** —¿De quién es el bolígrafo?
>
> —Es de Rosa.

C Walk around the classroom with a pencil and paper. Look for objects that you like and that belong to your classmates, and draw them as accurately as you can. Then get together with a partner and show him or her your drawings. Your partner tries to recognize the objects and say to whom they belong.

> **MODELO** —¿Es el lápiz de Manuela?
>
> —¡Sí! *or* No. Es el lápiz de Pablo.

Entre amigos

Everybody in the class should put something in a "lost-and-found" bag. It can be an article of clothing or some school item like a notebook or pen.

One student picks an item belonging to someone else from the bag and asks to whom it belongs: **¿De quién es (el suéter)?**

If someone tells them whose sweater it is **(Es de Alicia),** the student then hides the sweater, and asks Alicia questions to find out if it's hers:

> —Alicia, **¿de qué color es tu suéter? ¿Cómo es? ¿Es grande o pequeño? ¿Es bonito o feo?**

After Alicia answers the questions, the student shows her the sweater and asks, **Alicia, ¿es tu suéter?** Alicia will answer truthfully.

Take turns. See how quickly you can play the game.

En resumen

¿De quién es el lápiz?		
Es	**de**	David.
	del	alumno.
	de la	alumna.

¿De quién son los bolígrafos?		
Son	**de**	Sonia.
	del	alumno.
	de la	alumna.

¿De quiénes son los bolígrafos?		
Son	**de los**	alumnos.
	de las	alumnas.

¿Dónde se habla español?
México, Texas y El Álamo

Republic of Texas
Disputed land

Before 1840, most people in the United States lived east of the Mississippi River. Many people wanted to expand the United States by moving west. This movement was called Manifest Destiny. In 1835, Texas belonged to Mexico, but many U.S. citizens lived in the region. In October of that year, Sam Houston led a revolt against the Mexican government. General Santa Anna defended Mexico against Davy Crockett and Jim Bowie at the Alamo. Santa Anna won, but on April 21, 1836, the U.S. troops attacked him and his troops during their afternoon **siesta,** yelling, "Remember the Alamo!" Santa Anna lost this battle and was forced to sign a treaty giving Texas its independence from Mexico.

Datos

1815: Spain's holdings extend from the trans-Mississippi region south to Mexico and west to the Pacific. (This includes today's Texas, Arizona, New Mexico, California, Utah, Nevada, western Colorado and parts of Wyoming, Oklahoma and Kansas.)

1821: Mexico wins its independence from Spain and wins these lands. Mexico offers land in these territories to people willing to become Mexican citizens.

1829: The Mexican government abolishes slavery in Texas.

1835: Texans, under Sam Houston, rebel against Mexico. The Alamo at San Antonio falls to Mexican general Santa Anna. Davy Crockett and Jim Bowie die at the Alamo.

April 21, 1836: U.S. troops defeat Santa Anna and his troops at San Jacinto. Texas gains its independence.

1845: Texas is annexed to the United States.

1846–1848: War with Mexico

1848: Treaty of Guadalupe Hidalgo, which gives Mexico a total of $15,000,000 for Texas and its lands in the Southwest.

1853: Gadsden Purchase, giving Mexico $10,000,000 for additional lands in Arizona and New Mexico.

President Polk

General Taylor

¡Léelo en español!

La guerra con México En 1845, el presidente Polk de los Estados Unidos quiere la expansión[1] de los Estados Unidos hacia el oeste. Quiere más territorio para Texas. También quiere Nuevo México y California. El presidente Polk manda[1] al general Zachary Taylor al Río Grande. Esta acción no les gusta a los mexicanos, naturalmente[2]. En 1846 los soldados estadounidenses marchan a los territorios de Nuevo México y California y a México. En 1847 los estadounidenses ganan[3] a los mexicanos en estos territorios. El 2 de febrero de 1848 México y los Estados Unidos firman[4] el Tratado[5] de Guadalupe Hidalgo. Los estados de Arizona, Nuevo México, California, parte de Colorado y el resto de Texas pasan a ser[6] parte de los Estados Unidos. México recibe quince millones de dólares.

[1] sends [2] naturally [3] beat [4] sign [5] treaty
[6] become

Using What You Know What have you learned in your social studies class about Manifest Destiny? And about the war with Mexico? Discuss these events before reading the selection in Spanish.

Recognizing Cognates What do you think these words mean: **expansión, territorio, acción, marchan, resto?** Use these cognates to help you understand what is being said about the war with Mexico.

¡Comprendo!

Answer in English.

1. What president wanted to expand the territory of the United States?

2. How did the War with Mexico begin?

3. How long did the war last?

4. Who won the war?

5. What did each side win as a result of the war?

3

¿Cómo eres?

Kids sing at a community event.

Objetivos

- To talk about what you and others look like

- To talk about your personality and other people's

- To compare two people, places, or things

- To read about languages other than Spanish that are spoken in Latin America

Cuban friends
in La Habana

A man from
Ecuador

¿Sabías que...?

- As in the United States, people have moved to Latin America from different countries all over the world.

- Spanish isn't the only language spoken in Latin America.

- Many Latin Americans speak the languages their ancestors spoke before the Europeans came. One important example is the **quechua** language, spoken in parts of South America. Another is **guaraní,** an official language in Paraguay.

¿Cómo se dice?

¿Cómo son?

—¿Cómo son tus hermanos, Javier?

—Mi hermana Marisol es alta. Mi hermano Fernando es bajo y fuerte.

baja

débil

alta

fuerte

—¿Cómo es el pelo de tu prima?

—Es castaño y rizado.

rojizo　　　　**castaño**　　　　**rubio**　　　　**canoso**

ondulado　　　　**rizado**　　　　**lacio**

¿Sabías que...?

"Hispanic" (**hispano**) is a word used in the United States to refer to people from Latin American countries. They may also be the children or grandchildren of people who came from Latin America. That's one term for people from very different countries, cultures, and ethnic backgrounds! Some people prefer the term **Latino** to refer to their common roots.

¡Úsalo!

A Cut out six pictures of unknown people from magazines. Make sure they're not famous. Choose a secret name for each person and write it on the back. Show the pictures to your partner, who tries to guess the name you gave each person by asking questions like the ones below.

Partner A: Ask questions about each photo.

Partner B: Answer the questions.

> **MODELO** —¿Quién es alto?
>
> —Francisco es alto.

¿Quién tiene el pelo rubio?   ¿Quién es fuerte?

¿Quién tiene los ojos verdes?   ¿Quién es simpático(a)?

¿Quién tiene el pelo lacio?

B Get together with a partner. Take turns describing each person in the pictures. Don't forget to talk about their hair, their eyes, their height, etc. Together, write a description of one of the people. Read it to the class and see who's the first to guess which person is being described.

1.   2.   3.   4.   5.

Entre amigos

Find out if you and your classmates notice the same things about each other.

First work alone. Take a look around your class. Answer each question on the list with the name of a classmate who fits the description.

¿Quién es alto?

Francisco es alto.

Then compare each answer with those of your classmates. Did anyone have the same answer? Keep track. How many different answers did the class give for each question?

1. ¿Quién tiene el pelo castaño?
2. ¿Quién tiene los ojos azules?
3. ¿Quién es alto?
4. ¿Quién tiene los ojos castaños?
5. ¿Quién tiene el pelo lacio?
6. ¿Quién tiene el pelo rubio?
7. ¿Quién tiene el pelo rizado?
8. ¿Quién tiene el pelo rojizo?
9. ¿Quién tiene los ojos verdes?
10. ¿Quién tiene el pelo negro?

CONEXIÓN CON LAS MATEMÁTICAS

Fractions Complete a chart like this one about your classmates' hair and eye color by asking questions in Spanish and finding fractions. Write the fractions in their simplest form. What are the most common colors for hair and eyes? What is the most common type of hair? Make a bar graph showing your findings.

	Total de alumnos = 27	Fracción de la clase
Color de ojos		
azules	✔ ✔ ✔ = 3	$\frac{3}{27} = \frac{1}{9}$
castaños		
grises		
negros		
verdes		
Color de pelo		
castaño		
negro		
rojizo		
rubio		
Tipo de pelo		
corto		
largo		
lacio		
ondulado		
rizado		

◎ ◎ ◎ **Compara** ◎ ◎ ◎

En inglés	En español
type	el tipo
fraction	la fracción
total	el total

En resumen

alto	alta	¿Cómo **es** el pelo de tu prima?
bajo	baja	**Es** castaño y ondulado.
débil		rojizo rizado.
fuerte		rubio lacio.
		canoso.

¿Cómo se dice?

¡Qué simpático eres!

—Manuel es muy simpático, ¿verdad?

—Sí, es muy simpático.

—¿Y tú? ¿Eres simpático también?

—Sí, soy simpático.

simpático

atlética

inteligente

tímido

—¡Qué impaciente eres!

—¿Yo? Yo no soy impaciente.

impaciente

popular

generoso

cómica

¿Sabías que...?

Many people believe that you can tell what a person is like by the friends he or she has. In English we say: *Birds of a feather flock together.* In Spanish we say: **Dime con quién andas y te diré quién eres.** *(Tell me who you walk around with and I'll tell you who you are.)* Do you think this is true?

¡Úsalo!

A You're sending a family photo to your key pal in Nicaragua. Write a letter to accompany the photo. Be sure to describe each person in your family to your friend.

> **MODELO** El chico bajo y débil es mi hermano Tomás. Tomás es tímido.

B Get together with a partner and read the sentences below. Think about what kind of person is being described. Then choose a word from the box that fits the description. Remember that you may have to change the endings of some words.

generoso	impaciente	atlético
popular	simpático	tímido
inteligente	cómico	

> **MODELO** —A Susana le gusta dar (*give*) libros a sus amigos.
>
> —Ella es generosa.

1. Enrique tiene muchos amigos. A las personas les gusta mucho Enrique.

2. Eva estudia siempre. También aprende mucho.

3. Benito va a la clase de música ahora. Tiene mucha prisa.

4. Linda siempre practica deportes. Es muy fuerte.

5. Ramón no tiene miedo de hablar con las personas. A las personas les gusta mucho hablar con Ramón.

6. Alejandro tiene miedo de nadar. También tiene miedo de hablar con las personas.

¿Cómo son?

Entre amigos

Get together with four or five classmates. Write the names of three different famous people on slips of paper. You can use movie and TV stars, sports figures, politicians, or people you've learned about in social studies—even comic book or cartoon characters.

Put all the names in a bag. Take turns drawing one name at a time. Say as much as you can about the person whose name you draw. For example:

—**Supermán es popular y atlético. No es cómico. No es tímido.**

Your classmates tell you whether they agree or disagree with you.

En resumen

| Manuel es muy | atlético. |
| | simpático. |

Sí, soy	cómico.
	generoso.
	impaciente.
	popular.
	tímido.

¿Cómo se dice?

Talking about yourself and others

Here's how you tell what people are like.

Él **es** fuerte.   Ella **es** fuerte también.   Usted **es** muy fuerte.

Ellos **son** fuertes.   Ellas **son** fuertes también.

You use **es** when you're talking about one person and **son** when you're talking about more than one person. You have already been using these words to tell time and to name people and things. **Es** and **son** come from the verb **ser**.

By the way, did you notice that **fuerte** added an **-s** when it referred to more than one person?

Now look at these sentences. What word do you use to say what you are like? What word do you use to tell a friend what he or she is like?

Soy atlético.

Soy atlética.

Tú **eres** atlético.

Tú **eres** atlética.

When you talk about yourself and what you are like, use **soy.** You use **eres** when you want to tell a friend or family member what he or she is like. These words also come from the verb **ser.** Because these forms of **ser** tell who you're talking about, it's often unnecessary to use the words **yo, tú, él,** or **ella,** unless you want to make your meaning especially clear.

Notice that you use the word **atlético** to describe a boy. Use **atlética** to describe a girl.

You use words like **bajo, alto, simpático, generoso, tímido,** and **cómico** the same way.

¡Úsalo!

A Sometimes you can be rude, and it gets you into trouble! Work with a partner. Complete these sentences with **eres, es,** or **son** and say them to your partner. If you say something impolite, your partner calls you rude: **¡Qué maleducado(a)!**

> **MODELO** —¡Qué débil eres tú!
>
> —¡Qué maleducado! *or* ¡Qué maleducada!

1. Señora, ¡qué fuerte _____ usted!

2. ¡Qué inteligentes _____ Ángela y Laura!

3. ¡Qué cómico _____ Gregorio!

4. ¡Qué fuerte _____ tú!

5. Señor, ¡qué débil _____ usted!

6. ¡Qué bajos _____ Francisco y Guillermo!

7. ¡Qué alta _____ Esperanza!

8. ¡Qué impaciente _____ Horacio!

B Read these questions from a letter written by your Spanish-speaking key pal. Then answer them by describing yourself in a letter. Choose the part of the question that's right for you.

> **MODELO** ¿Eres alto? / ¿Eres alta?
>
> **Sí, soy alto.** *or* **No, no soy alto.**
>
> **Sí, soy alta.** *or* **No, no soy alta.**

1. ¿Eres simpático? / ¿Eres simpática?

2. ¿Eres tímido? / ¿Eres tímida?

3. ¿Eres atlético? / ¿Eres atlética?

4. ¿Eres generoso? / ¿Eres generosa?

5. ¿Eres cómico? / ¿Eres cómica?

C Write a description of yourself on a card, but don't write your name on it. It should be about five sentences long. Write your initials in the corner. Give your card to your teacher.

 **Soy alto y fuerte. Tengo el pelo rojizo y rizado. Tengo los ojos azules. Soy inteligente y tímido. No soy atlético.**

Your teacher will mix all the cards together and then give each of you a card to read aloud. Use **es** and **tiene** to describe him or her. Try to guess the person's name.

D Talk about the people in this picture with a partner. Take turns asking and answering questions. Make guesses about these people's personalities. Use these sample questions and make up some of your own.

1. ¿Quiénes tienen el pelo canoso?
2. ¿Cuántas chicas hay? ¿Cuántos chicos hay?
3. ¿Cuántas personas tienen el pelo castaño?
4. ¿Son simpáticos los chicos?
5. ¿Es alta o baja la señora del vestido morado?
6. ¿Cuántos años tiene el chico de la camisa azul?

Entre amigos

With your partner, choose a favorite TV show. It should be about a family or a group of people who are often together. Think of at least three characters who appear in the show.

Divide a sheet of paper into three or more columns (one for each character). Do this across the long side of the sheet. In each column, write as many sentences as you can describing the character. Don't reveal the character's name!

Here's an example from *The Simpsons.*

Es un hombre.
Es alto y amarillo.
No tiene pelo.
Es impaciente.
Es cómico.
No es atlético.
No es tímido.

Present your descriptions to the class. See if your classmates can guess who the characters are before you tell their names. Can they? Do they know what show you're talking about?

La persona se llama Homer Simpson.

En resumen

(Yo)	**Soy**	
(Tú)	**Eres**	atlético / atlética.
(Él, Ella, Ud.)	**Es**	
(Ellos, Ellas)	**Son**	fuertes.

¿Cómo se dice?

Making comparisons

Study these pictures and sentences. What words do you use to compare two people, places, or things?

Juan

César

Juan es alto. César es **más** alto **que** Juan.

Emilia

Carmen

Emilia es simpática. Carmen es **más** simpática **que** Emilia.

mi gato

tu gato

Mi gato es grande. Tu gato es **menos** grande **que** mi gato.

mi abrigo

tu abrigo

Mi abrigo es largo. Tu abrigo es **menos** largo **que** mi abrigo.

To give the idea of "more than" in Spanish—for example, "more impatient than" or "taller than"—use **más... que.**

To give the idea of "less than," use **menos... que.**

¡Úsalo!

Get together with a partner and look at the pictures. Ask each other questions to compare these people.

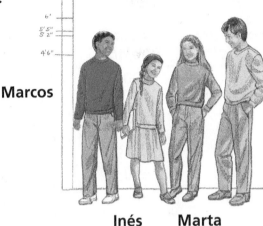

Marcos

Ramón

Inés   **Marta**

MODELO —¿Quién es más baja que Marta?

—Inés es más baja que Marta.

Entre amigos

Work with five or six classmates. Compare pairs of things or famous people. One person names an object or a famous person. A second person names another object or another famous person.

Everyone then has one minute to write a sentence comparing the two objects or people using **más... que** or **menos... que.** Are the comparisons correct? Compare your group's work with the other groups.

el globo—el escritorio
El escritorio es más grande que el globo.

Michael Jordan—Troy Aikman
Michael Jordan es menos fuerte que Troy Aikman.

CONEXIÓN CON LAS MATEMÁTICAS

Comparing Measurements

Look at the heights and weights of several different animals. Work with a partner and make as many comparisons as you can between the animals on this list.

Animal	Altura (Height)	Longitud (Length)	Peso (Weight)	¿Cómo es?
jirafa	5 m		1200 kg	tímida, muy alta
oso	2 m		350 kg	fuerte, muy grande
tigre		2 m	160 kg	fuerte, grande
pez		7 cm	50 g	tímido, muy pequeño
loro		60 cm	650 g	cómico, muy inteligente
gato		85 cm	9 kg	inteligente, no muy atlético, muy gordo
ratón		15 cm	300 g	simpático, pequeño
perro	70 cm		30 kg	muy simpático
delfín	3.5 m		500 kg	muy inteligente

☉ ☉ ☉ Compara ☉ ☉ ☉

En inglés	En español
giraffe	la jirafa
dolphin	el delfín

¿Sabías que...?

Spanish has adopted several animal words from the **guaraní** language of Paraguay, such as **jaguar, ñandú** (a type of ostrich), **tapir, tucán** (*toucan*) and **yacaré** (*alligator*). As you can see, some of these words have made it into the English language as well!

Entre amigos

Get in a group of four or five classmates to play this matching game. Before you start, make two sets of cards with all the descriptive words you learned in this unit. Also make five cards with **menos... que** and five cards with **más... que** on them.

Spread out the word cards facedown on a desk. Then mix the **más / menos** cards, and put them facedown in a pile.

One person starts by picking up two of the word cards from the desk. If they don't match, he or she puts them back facedown in their original positions, and the turn passes to the next player. If they do match, that player then picks a card from the **más / menos** pile. He or she makes a sentence with the word on the two word cards and the comparison phrase.

If the other players agree that the sentence is correct, the first player keeps the two word cards. Otherwise, they go back down on the table. Then it's the next player's turn.

Keep playing until there are no more word cards left on the table. The player with the most cards at the end is the winner.

En resumen

César es	**más**			Juan.
		alto	**que**	
Juan es	**menos**			César.

¿Dónde se habla español?

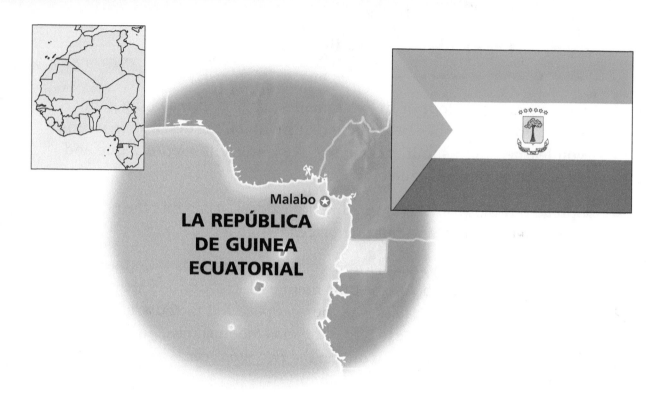

Malabo ☆

LA REPÚBLICA DE GUINEA ECUATORIAL

La República de Guinea Ecuatorial

Equatorial Guinea is made up of two provinces, Río Muni and Bioko. The country is found between Cameroon and Gabon, in the continent of Africa.

It also includes the islands of Bioko, Annobón, Corisco, Elobey Grande, and Elobey Chico.

Datos

Capital: Malabo

Ciudades importantes: Bata

Idiomas: Español, francés, dialectos africanos, inglés

Moneda: El franco CFA

Población: 510,000

leña

¡Léelo en español!

La gente de la República de Guinea Ecuatorial La gente de Río Muni, de la República de Guinea Ecuatorial es parte de la familia bantu. Se llaman los fang. Los fang cazan[1] y cultivan[2] productos como batatas[3], yucas y bananas. Exportan leña y café.

La gente de la isla de Bioko son los bubi. Ellos son principalmente agricultores[4] con fincas[5] pequeñas. Venden sus productos al mercado. La religión de la mayoría[6] de la gente es católica.

Su capital, Malabo, está en la isla de Bioko. Exportan cacao, un ingrediente importante para el chocolate.

El explorador Fernando Pó de Portugal llegó[7] a Bioko en el siglo XV. Los españoles gobernaron[8] el país hasta 1968, cuando Guinea Ecuatorial ganó[9] su independencia.

café

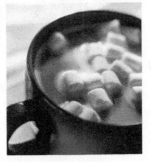

cacao

[1] hunt   [2] grow   [3] sweet potatoes   [4] farmers
[5] farms   [6] majority   [7] arrived   [8] governed
[9] won

Reading Strategy

Skimming Read quickly through the passage. Underline or make a list of the words you do not know. Can you guess what they might mean? Check their meanings in a dictionary. Now read the passage again.

Recognizing Cognates What do you think these words mean: **principalmente, católica, exportan, ingrediente, explorador, independencia?** Use these cognates to help you understand what is being said about Equatorial Guinea.

¡Comprendo!

Answer in English.

1. Find Equatorial Guinea on a globe. Describe its location. Point to all the countries that share a border with Equatorial Guinea.

2. What are the two main provinces and what products does each export?

3. Who are the Fang and the Bubi peoples?

4. Who was the first European to land in Equatorial Guinea?

UNIDAD
4

¿Cómo es tu casa?

Objetivos

- To name the outside parts of a home
- To name the rooms of a home
- To talk about more than one person, place, or thing at a time
- To talk about where people, places, and things are
- To compare houses and buildings in different places

These white houses are typical in the south of Spain.

Balconies decorate these homes in San Juan, Puerto Rico.

Interior of a colonial house in Cienfuegos, Cuba.

¿Sabías que...?

- The word **casa** can mean both "house" and "home."

- Many Latin American and Spanish homes have wrought-iron bars **(las rejas)** in windows and balconies. Their beautiful latticework decorates and protects homes.

- When Spanish-speaking people want to make you feel at home, they say **Mi casa es tu casa.**

¿Cómo se dice?

¿Qué hay fuera de la casa?

 —¿Cómo es tu casa?

—Bueno, mi casa es muy bonita.

—¿Tiene patio?

—¡Claro que sí!

el techo

la chimenea

el patio

el jardín

el balcón

el garaje

las escaleras
gradas

el buzón

la cerca

¡Úsalo!

A These pictures are similar, but there are seven differences! Work with a partner to find them. Each of you chooses one of the scenes and covers the other one with a sheet of paper. Then describe what you see to find the differences.

MODELO —Hay un balcón.

—Hay dos balcones.

CONEXIÓN CON LOS **ESTUDIOS SOCIALES**

Spanish Missions Spanish missionaries in Latin America built missions with materials like adobe, brick, tile, and stone. Much of it was covered with plaster and whitewashed. Missions consisted of some low, simple buildings surrounding a **patio,** with corridors supported by arches outside and inside. Do you know of any famous missions?

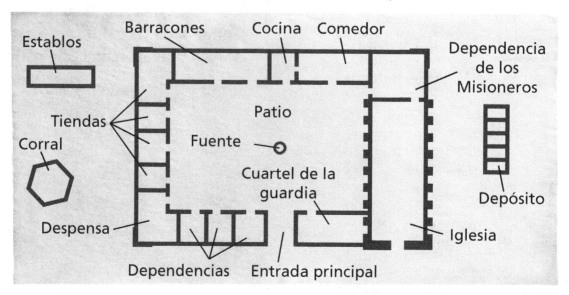

B Imagine your dream home. Draw and color it. Include all the parts of the house you know in Spanish. Then get together with a partner and ask each other questions about your dream homes. Make a drawing of your partner's house based on his or her answers, and see if your drawing matches your partner's!

MODELO —¿Hay _____ en la casa?

—¿De qué color son _____ de la casa?

—¿Cuántos _____ hay?

—¿Cómo es _____?

Entre amigos

Draw and color your own house or apartment building (**el apartamento**) as seen from the outside. Draw it big! Label the parts you've learned in this chapter.

You also know some other Spanish words you can use for labels on your house or apartment. You can label the doors and windows, for example. Are there any other words you've learned that will work as labels?

Now form a group of four or five classmates. Show your picture and point out the labels. Tell the group as much as you can about your house or building. Answer any questions they have about it. Be ready to ask them questions about their pictures.

Here are some sample questions you might ask each other:

¿Cuántas puertas tiene tu casa?
¿Cuál es el número de tu apartamento?
¿De qué color es el techo de tu casa?
¿Tu apartamento es grande o pequeño?
¿Tiene escaleras tu casa?

En resumen

el balcón	la cerca
el buzón	la chimenea
el garaje	las escaleras
el jardín	
el patio	
el techo	

¿Cómo se dice?

¿Qué hay dentro de la casa?

—¿Cuántos cuartos tiene tu casa?

—Tiene seis.

—¿Es grande la cocina?

—No, es mediana. Pero es bonita.

Los cuartos

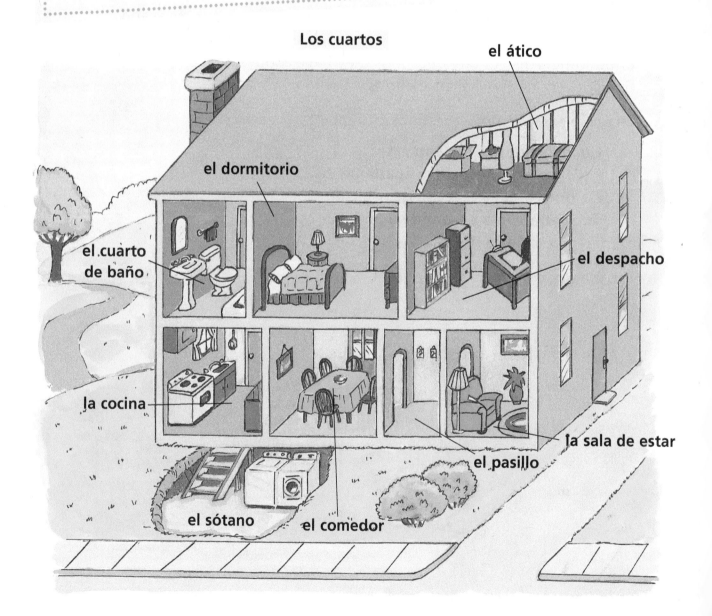

el ático

el dormitorio

el cuarto
de baño

el despacho

la cocina

el sótano

el comedor

el pasillo

la sala de estar

—¿Dónde está el señor Gómez?

—Está dentro de la casa.

—¿Y su perro? ¿Dónde está?

—Está fuera de la casa.

 ## CONEXIÓN CON LAS MATEMÁTICAS

Area You need to help your mom set up her office. Get to work! First, you need to paint the walls. Estimate the length and height of each wall. Figure out the total area of the walls. One gallon of paint covers 400–500 square feet. How much paint will you need?

Now get together with a partner and compare how much paint you each need. Then compare the sizes of the rooms.

MODELO —**Voy a comprar dos galones. El despacho de mi mamá es más grande que el despacho de tu mamá.**

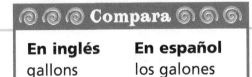

En inglés	En español
gallons	los galones

¡Úsalo!

A Your family wants to rent out your home. Describe your own house or apartment to a partner using all the vocabulary you know. Your partner writes an ad for the newspaper.

Now get together with two other pairs. Look at all the ads and decide where you would choose to live.

Apartamento

El apartamento es grande. Tiene tres dormitorios y un cuarto de baño grande. Hay una cocina nueva. No hay garaje. Hay dos balcones pequeños. Las paredes son blancas.

B Sometimes the García house is like a zoo! Look at the picture of their house and write five true or false sentences about it. Use **dentro** and **fuera**. Then get together with a partner and read each sentence. Your partner has to figure out if it's true **(verdadero)** or false **(falso).** If it's false, your partner needs to make it true.

MODELO —El oso está dentro de la casa.

—Falso. El oso está fuera de la casa.

1. el Sr. García
2. Tonio el tigre
3. Luisa
4. el perro
5. la Sra. García
6. el pájaro

CONEXIÓN CON LAS MATEMÁTICAS

Perimeter Look at this plan of a house and find the perimeter of each room. Check your answers with a partner. Take turns comparing the perimeters of the rooms using **corto** and **largo**.

MODELO **El comedor tiene un perímetro de 13 metros. El perímetro del comedor es menos largo que el perímetro del dormitorio uno.**

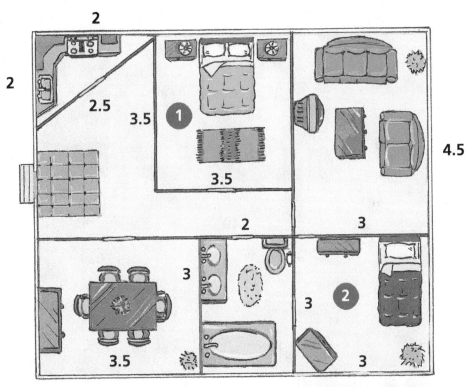

En resumen

el ático	el dormitorio	la cocina
el comedor	el pasillo	la sala de estar
el cuarto de	el sótano	dentro de
baño	los cuartos	fuera de
el despacho		

◎ ◎ ◎ Compara ◎ ◎ ◎

En inglés	En español
meter	el metro
perimeter	el perímetro

¿Cómo se dice?

Talking about more than one person

Do you remember how to say "I," "you," "he," and "she"?

yo

tú

usted

él

ella

Now here are the words that mean "we," "you" (when there's more than one person), and "they."

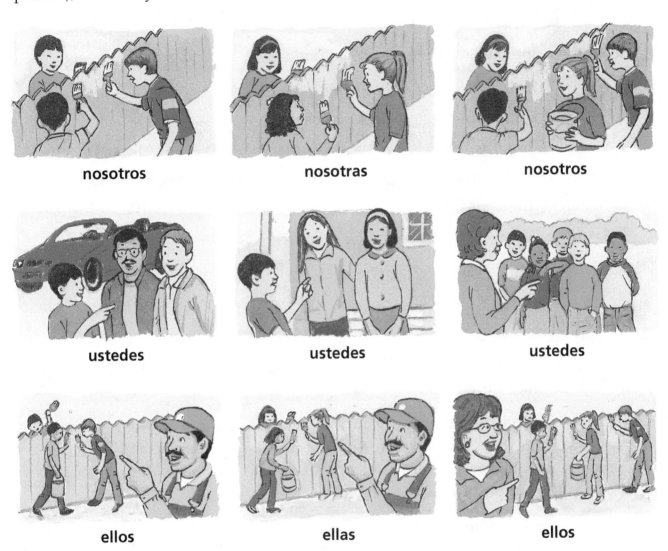

nosotros

nosotras

nosotros

ustedes

ustedes

ustedes

ellos

ellas

ellos

Use **nosotros** and **ellos** when you're talking about more than one male, or any time there is at least one male in a group. Use **nosotras** and **ellas** when there are *only* females in a group. **Ustedes** stays the same in all cases.

Elena, Tomás y yo (chico) = nosotros
Sandra, Eva y yo (chica) = nosotras
Raúl, María y usted = ustedes
Raúl, María y tú = ustedes
Raúl, María y Elena = ellos
María, Elena y Sandra = ellas

¡Úsalo!

A Solve these "problems." Then compare your answers with a partner.

> **MODELO** Javier + Lina + Sonia = ellos
>
> Lola + Tina + yo (Isabel) = nosotras

1. Elena + Carlota + Ana = _____
2. María + Julia + yo (Alicia) = _____
3. Sr. Fonseca + Sra. Bolívar = _____
4. Berta + Javier + yo (Eduardo) = _____
5. Samuel + tú (Ricardo) = _____
6. Manuel + Raúl + yo (Paco) = _____
7. Carlos + Paula + yo (Lisa) = _____
8. Eva + Sandra + tú (Rosa) = _____
9. Sr. García + Ud. = _____

B Form a circle with five classmates. Write your name on a card, mix all the cards up, and put them facedown.

Take turns picking out three cards. Read the names out loud and have those people stand up. Ask the person to your right who these people are. The person answers with **ellos** or **ellas.** If the person answering is also standing, he or she uses **nosotros** or **nosotras.**

> **MODELO** —¿Quiénes son?
>
> —¡Son ellas! *or* ¡Son ellos! *or* ¡Somos nosotros! *or* ¡Somos nosotras!

¿Sabías que...?

Most people in Latin American cities used to live in small houses or in two- or three-story apartment buildings. But with millions of people moving into large cities over the last fifty years, there are now high-rise apartment buildings all over Latin America.

Entre amigos

Time for a round of "Think Fast!" Your teacher will have you and your classmates stand in different places around the classroom. Some of you will be in groups or pairs, and some will be alone. Your teacher will give each student, pair, or group a piece of paper in different colors. One student will get a foam ball.

Now the game begins! Your teacher asks a question about color like this: **¿Quién tiene el rojo?** The student with the ball tosses it to another student who must answer with a word like **yo, ellos,** or **nosotros.** The answer depends on who has that colored paper.

Think fast! Whoever answers incorrectly or takes more than five seconds must sit down.

¿Sabías que...?

House styles and building materials vary widely in the Spanish-speaking world. In the tropics, houses are often built of cement and tile to keep them cool and withstand frequent hurricanes. In Puerto Rico, windows have built-in shutters that can be closed to protect windows from strong winds.

En resumen

Yo
Tú
Usted
Él
Ella
Nosotros (Raúl + Silvia + yo [Marta])
Nosotras (Sonia + Silvia + yo [Marta])
Ustedes
Ellos   (Raúl + Silvia + Marta)
Ellas   (Sonia + Silvia + Marta)

¿Cómo se dice?

Where are they?

Look at these pictures and sentences to see how to talk about where people are.

Singular	**Plural**

Estoy en la casa.

Estamos en la casa.

Estás en la casa.

Están en la casa.

Está en la casa.

Están en la casa.

You can also use **está** and **están** to talk about where places and things are located. All of these forms come from the verb **estar.**

If you want to ask where someone or something is, you ask **¿Dónde... ?**

—**¿Dónde están** Julia y Margarita?

—**Están** en el jardín.

—**¿Dónde está** el perro?

—**Está** en la cocina.

¡Úsalo!

A With a partner, choose two tasks done in different rooms in a house—for example, cooking in the kitchen or vacuuming in the living room. Then get together with two more pairs and take turns acting out your tasks. The other pairs ask questions to guess where you are. Who can guess fastest?

> **MODELO** —Pedro y Gloria, ¿están en el sótano?
>
> —No, no estamos en el sótano.
>
> —¿Están en la cocina?
>
> —Sí, estamos en la cocina.

CONEXIÓN CON LOS ESTUDIOS SOCIALES

Pueblos The Pueblo are a Native American group living in compact villages (**pueblos**) that look like apartment buildings, made out of adobe or stone. They have been building these structures for over a thousand years. Originally, the entrance was a hole in the roof and there were no windows.

A.

Get together with a partner and compare the **pueblo** with this unusual apartment building in Barcelona.

> **MODELO** En la A, las paredes son de color marrón. En la B, las paredes son...

B.

Now compare both of these buildings to an apartment building you know.

B Work with a partner and describe this strange house. When your teacher says **¡Ahora!,** write a list of sentences describing where these people and things are. Stop when your teacher says **¡Alto!** Which pair came up with the most sentences? Hints: You'll need to use **estar.** And don't forget **dentro** and **fuera.**

CONEXIÓN CON LA SALUD

Fire Safety Do you know what to do in case of fire? Every family should have an escape plan to safely get everyone outside of the house as quickly as possible.

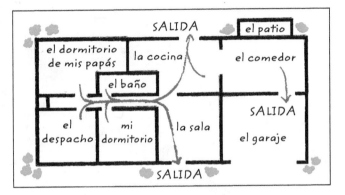

The smoke from a fire can make it hard to see where things are. It's important to learn and remember the different ways out of your home. Planning ahead saves lives!

Draw a plan of your house. Include all the floors and all the rooms. Label the rooms and then label all the possible exits: **SALIDA.** Then draw an escape route from every room. Remember the exact routes!

Get together with a partner and exchange drawings. Your partner mentions a room. You say the places you need to go through to get out of the house from that room. Your partner follows the route on your drawing to see if you remember your house's plan.

Partner A: Say your partner is in a room and ask where the exit is.

Partner B: Say where the nearest exit is and the places you need to go through in order to get out.

MODELO —Estás en el dormitorio. ¿Dónde está la salida?

—La salida está en la cocina. Voy al pasillo. Voy a las escaleras...

En resumen

	estar
(Yo)	estoy
(Tú)	estás
(Él, Ella, Ud.)	está
(Nosotros, Nosotras)	estamos
(Ellos, Ellas, Uds.)	están

¿Dónde se habla español?

EL SALVADOR
San Salvador

El Salvador

El Salvador was inhabited by the Olmec people as early as 2,000 B.C. Although a very destructive civil war ravaged the country from 1980 to 1992, today El Salvador has one of the strongest economies of Latin America. It exports coffee, sugar, and textiles. Many Salvadorians live and work in the United States and send money home.

El Salvador has many natural parks and preserves you can explore, and the government is taking steps to protect the country's plants and wildlife.

In El Salvador, **el almuerzo** is the largest meal of the day. A typical food sold everywhere is **pupusas.** These are made of cornmeal and stuffed with cheese, refried beans or pork rinds. **Licuados** are also very popular; these are drinks made of blended fruit. A typical souvenir are **sorpresas** (literally, "surprises"), which are little scenes created inside a shell.

◎ ◎ ◎ ◎ Datos ◎ ◎ ◎ ◎

Capital: San Salvador

Ciudades importantes: San Miguel, Santa Ana

Idiomas: Español, náhuatl

Moneda: El dólar estadounidense

Población: 6.5 millones

pupusas

¡Léelo en español!

Caminar y practicar el surfing

En El Salvador, se puede apreciar la naturaleza. Dos actividades para apreciar la naturaleza son caminar en los parques y practicar el surfing en la playa. En el Parque Nacional Montecristo-El Trifinio, se puede dar un paseo y mirar los pájaros en un bosque nubloso[1] de las montañas. En el Parque Nacional El Imposible, se puede caminar en un bosque original y ver muchas especies de plantas y animales en peligro de extinción.[2] También se puede caminar en la Ruta de las Flores para ver las plantas de café. O tal vez[3] prefieres dar un paseo en el parque Cerro Verde para ver el volcán Izalco.

Otra actividad especial en El Salvador es el surfing. En La Libertad se puede buscar la ola[4] perfecta. En la Costa del Bálsamo hay más oportunidades para el surf. El Salvador es un buen lugar para gozar de[5] la naturaleza.

[1] cloud forest [2] endangered [3] maybe [4] wave [5] enjoy

¡Comprendo!

Answer in English.

1. If you were to go hiking in El Salvador, where would you go? What would you expect to see?

2. What are some places people go to surf in El Salvador?

3. Why do you think El Salvador uses the U.S. dollar as its national currency?

4. What might be some of the ways in which the Salvadoran government is trying to protect endangered plant and animal life?

5

Dentro de tu casa

Objetivos

- To talk about your living room and bedroom
- To learn more ways to describe people, places, and things
- To describe where something is located
- To learn more about homes in Spanish-speaking countries

Interior of a guesthouse in Bogotá, Colombia

Anteroom in Guatemalan home

Four girls have a slumber party

¿Sabías que...?

- Because of satellite dishes and cable TV, people in Latin America and Spain may be watching some of the same programs you are.

- In Spanish-speaking countries, coffee is often served in the living room when guests come over to someone's house. It's sometimes served in sets of small cups reserved for guests only!

- To keep cool in the tropics, houses have terraces and rooms that are open to the outside. Wrought-iron bars keep people out, but birds, lizards, and other small animals may show up in your living room once in a while!

¿Cómo se dice?

¿Qué hay en la sala de estar?

—¿Qué hay en la sala de estar de tu casa?

—Hay un sofá, un televisor, una alfombra y mucho más.

el retrato

el techo

las cortinas

el estéreo

el televisor

la videocasetera

la alfombra

la lámpara

el piso

los muebles

—Mamá, ¿dónde está mi libro de español?

—Está en la estantería.

el sofá

el sillón

el lector de DVD

la estantería

el estante

—¿Cómo es el sillón?

—Es nuevo.

nuevo

viejo

¡Úsalo!

A Draw a floor plan of your house or an imaginary one. Be sure to include all the rooms! Use this floor plan as a guide, but don't add labels.

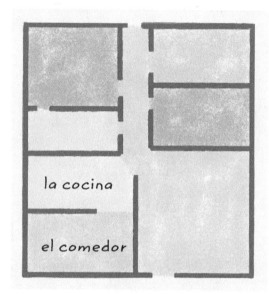

Get together with a partner and explain which room is which. Your partner labels the rooms.

Then your partner asks you where the furniture and other items are. He or she will ask about the items on the list below and think of others. As you describe their location, your partner draws them on the floor plan. Check for accuracy. Then switch roles.

MODELO —¿Dónde están tus libros?

—Mis libros están en la sala de estar, en un estante.

los libros	el sofá	el televisor	la computadora
los retratos	las cortinas	la videocasetera	el estéreo

B Make a list of things in your home that are old and things that are new.

MODELO El televisor es viejo. El lector de DVD es nuevo.

Now get together with a partner. Imagine that you have a million dollars. Tell your partner which things you will replace in your home.

MODELO —Voy a comprar un televisor grande.

Area Choose one of these diagrams as your living room. You need to buy wall-to-wall carpeting. Look at the size of the square tiles in your room. Find the area of the floor so you know how much carpeting to buy.

 50 cm

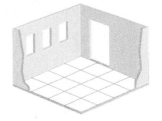 30 cm

 20 cm

Now get together with two other classmates who chose other diagrams. Compare how much carpeting each of you needs.

MODELO —¿**Cuántos metros de alfombra vas a comprar?**

Based on your answers, compare your rooms and say which one is larger and which one is smaller than the other.

MODELO —**La sala de estar de Roberto es más grande que la sala de estar de Luis.**

◎ ◎ ◎ **Compara** ◎ ◎ ◎

En inglés	En español
centimeter	el centímetro
meter	el metro

En resumen

el lector de DVD	nuev**o**	**la** alfombra	nuev**a**
el estante	viej**o**	**la** estantería	viej**a**
el estéreo	el sofá	la lámpara	
el piso	el techo	la videocasetera	
el retrato	el televisor		
el sillón		**las** cortinas	nuev**as**
			viej**as**
los muebles	nuev**os**		
	viej**os**		

¿Cómo se dice?

¿Qué hay en tu dormitorio?

—¿Qué hay en tu dormitorio?

—Mi cama, ¡claro! Y todas mis cosas favoritas.

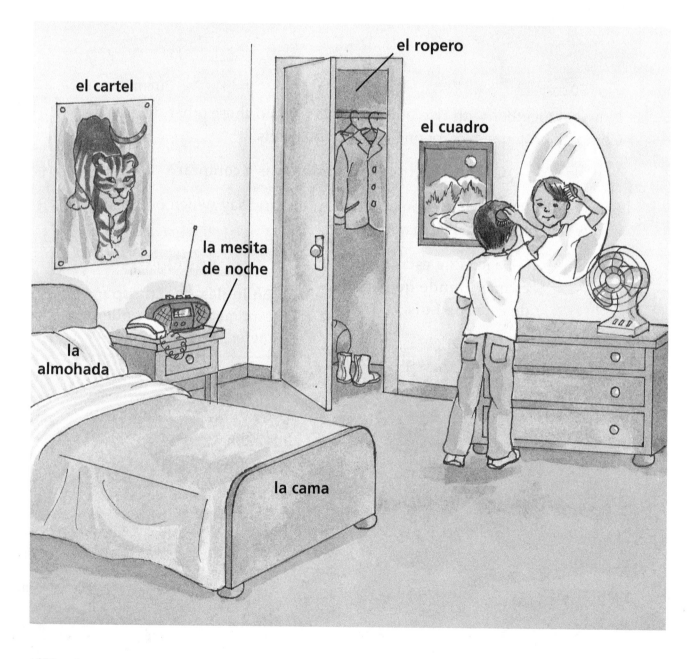

el ropero

el cartel

el cuadro

la mesita de noche

la almohada

la cama

—¿Dónde está tu radio?

—Está en la mesita de noche.

el espejo

el radio

el tocador

La Comoda

el ventilador

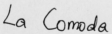

CONEXIÓN CON LOS ESTUDIOS SOCIALES

Arab Influence Spanish is not the only language that has been spoken in Spain. For many centuries, Spain was home to the Moors, who ruled and lived in the region for 800 years. Their influence can be seen on Spanish buildings, in art, and even in the language! Most words that start with **al-** in Spanish come from Arabic. What words in Spanish do you know that came from Arabic?

¡Úsalo!

A Look at these four rooms. Choose one secretly and write a description of it. Write everything you can about it.

Then get together with three or four classmates. Read your description to them and have them guess which room you picked. They should let you finish before guessing.

> **MODELO** **Hay una cama blanca con dos almohadas...**

B Form a group with three or four classmates. Take turns describing your bedrooms or imaginary ones. Say what's in the bedroom and where each item is.

> **MODELO** —**Tengo una cama grande y dos almohadas. También tengo una mesita de noche. Hay una lámpara en la mesita. Tengo cuatro carteles. Están en las paredes...**

Draw rooms based on your classmates' descriptions. Then show them the drawings to see if they are accurate.

C Get together with a partner. Imagine that this is a floor plan of your partner's new apartment. Your partner needs help decorating!

Help by saying what he or she needs (use **necesitas)** in each room and what to buy. Be specific and creative with your suggestions! Your partner draws the furniture that you suggest and that he or she likes.

MODELO —No hay camas. En el dormitorio necesitas una cama. En la sala de estar necesitas un sofá. ¿Vas a comprar un sofá blanco y negro?

En resumen

el cartel	la almohada
el cuadro	la cama
el espejo	la mesita de noche
el radio	
el ropero	
el tocador	
el ventilador	

¿Cómo se dice?

Where is it?

Read the sentences below. Which words tell you that a person or thing is close to something? Which words tell you that a person or thing is far from something?

El niño está **cerca de** la lámpara.

La niña está **lejos de** la lámpara.

Now read the sentences below these pictures. Which words tell you that a person or thing is in front of something? Which words tell you that a person or thing is behind something?

El niño está **delante del** sofá.

La niña está **detrás del** sofá.

In the last unit, you learned **dentro de** and **fuera de** to talk about people or things being inside or outside the house. **Cerca de, lejos de, delante de,** and **detrás de** work the same way.

Remember that when **de** comes before **el,** the two words become **del.**

¡Úsalo!

A Play a guessing game! Get together with a partner. Secretly choose an item or a person in your classroom and write down the word or name. Give one clue at a time about the item's or person's location. Your partner may ask you questions. Then it's your turn to guess!

> **MODELO** —Está cerca de las ventanas.
>
> —¿Está lejos del pizarrón?

B Look at the items in this living room for one minute. Then close your book and get together with a partner. Your partner looks at the book and asks you where different things are. Use **cerca de, lejos de, delante de,** or **detrás de** to answer. Remember to use **del,** if needed. Your partner helps you if you don't remember. Then switch roles.

> **MODELO** —¿Dónde está el sillón?
>
> —El sillón está cerca del sofá. Está delante de la pared.

C Pick a partner and find out about his or her house! Write down at least five questions about where things are in the living room or bedroom. Here are some examples:

MODELO ¿Qué está cerca del televisor? ¿Tienes un cuadro en tu dormitorio? ¿Dónde está... ?

Ask and answer each other's questions. Then draw your partner's living room or bedroom based on his or her descriptions. Show your drawing to your partner to see if it's accurate!

Entre amigos

Play **Araña, araña** (*Spider, spider*).

A spider is hiding in your classroom! Write the hiding place on a slip of paper, but don't show it to anyone. Let's say you decide the spider is hiding **detrás del escritorio.**

Play the game with a classmate, who must find the spider. The classmate names locations, and you answer, as if you were the spider.

—**Araña, araña, ¿estás aquí?**

—**¿Dónde?**

—**Cerca del mapa.**

—**No, no estoy cerca del mapa.**

When your partner says **Detrás del escritorio.** you say **¡Sí!** and show your partner the slip of paper. Then switch roles. Whoever finds the spider with the fewest guesses wins the game.

Geography Look at this map of Latin America for three minutes. Try to remember where each country (**país**) is located in relation to the others. Is it near or far?

Now close your book. Your partner will choose a country and ask for countries that are close to it and far from it. Answer according to what you remember.

MODELO

—¿Qué país está cerca de Argentina?

—Mm... Chile está cerca de Argentina.

—¿Qué país está lejos de Argentina?

—Mm... México está lejos de Argentina.

If you're right, your partner asks you more questions. If you're wrong, your partner gives you the correct answer, and it's your turn to ask your own questions.

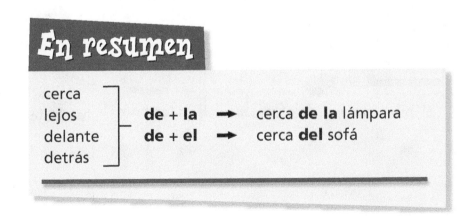

En resumen

cerca		
lejos	**de + la** →	cerca **de la** lámpara
delante	**de + el** →	cerca **del** sofá
detrás		

Lección 4

¿Cómo se dice?

Talking about people, places, and things

Since you began studying Spanish, you've used many words for people, places, and things. Some of these are:

el espejo	**la cocina**	**la sala de estar**
el sótano	**la cama**	**la alumna**
el alumno		

Have you wondered why some words use **el** and others **la?**

In English, you think only of people and animals as being masculine (male) or feminine (female). In Spanish, however, all nouns are either masculine or feminine—even words for places and things. **El** words are called "masculine," and **la** words are called "feminine." When you're talking about more than one, it's the same thing: **los** words are masculine, and **las** words are feminine.

Usually, masculine words end in **-o,** and feminine words end in **-a.** This isn't always true, though. So the best way to know is to learn the word together with its article, **el** or **la.**

MASCULINO   FEMENINO

el vestido   el televisor   el teléfono   la lámpara   las botas   la camisa

This masculine-feminine difference is important when you're using descriptive words to talk about people, places, or things.

El día es **fresco.**

La noche es **bonita.**

Los días de invierno son **fríos.**

¡Las noches de verano son **fantásticas!**

If the word is masculine, the word describing it must be masculine, too. If the word is feminine, the descriptive word must be feminine. If the word is plural (that is, if there's more than one), the descriptive word must also be plural.

The only exceptions are descriptive words like **gris** and **grande** that don't end in **-o** or **-a.** These words stay the same for masculine and feminine words. But they do add an **-s** or **-es** in the plural.

¡Úsalo!

A Get together with a partner. Ask your partner questions about the clothing he or she has at home. What color are his or her clothes? Are they new or old? Big or small? Are they short or long? Based on the answers, give your partner a list of things he or she might need to replace soon. Use the items of clothing on the list or other items that you know in Spanish.

MODELO —¿La bata es nueva o vieja? ¿De qué color es?

| los calcetines | las botas | la chaqueta | el traje de baño | los zapatos |
| las camisetas | la falda | el abrigo | los pantalones | la bata |

—Es nueva. *or* No tengo una bata.

B Make a poster of your dream room! Get together with two classmates and decide whether to decorate a bedroom or a living room. Look through catalogs and magazines to find the different items you will need for your room.

When you find something you like, ask each of your classmates if they like it and to tell you why. If they both like it, cut it out to add to your dream room.

MODELO —¿Te gusta el tocador negro?

—No, no me gusta. Es feo. *or* Sí, me gusta. Es grande.

CONEXIÓN CON LAS MATEMÁTICAS

Percent Make a list of the furniture in your bedroom using a chart like this one. Add other items if you like.

	Color	Grande / Pequeño	Viejo / Nuevo	Feo / Bonito
el tocador				
las sillas				
el ropero				
las cortinas				
la alfombra				
la mesita de noche				
la lámpara				

Now get together with a partner and compare your furniture.

MODELO **El tocador es marrón. Es más grande que el tocador de José. No tengo una mesita de noche...**

Join two more pairs and add up all your items. Which ones are the same? Figure out what the percentage is of these items.

MODELO **El cincuenta por ciento de los tocadores son marrones.**

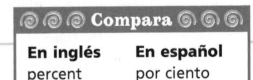

Compara

En inglés	En español
percent	por ciento

En resumen

Masculino
el día ➞ fresc**o**
los días ➞ frí**os**

Femenino
la noche ➞ bonit**a**
las noches ➞ fantástic**as**

¿Dónde se habla español?

CHILE

Santiago ✪

Chile

(República de Chile)

Chile is 4,630 kilometers long. It stretches from Peru to the Strait of Magellan. Within its borders you will find many natural wonders: the Andes mountains, the driest desert in the world, volcanoes, sparkling blue and green lakes, geysers, glaciers, and the region of Patagonia.

Datos

Capital: Santiago

Ciudades importantes: Antofagasta, Concepción, Valparaíso, Viña del Mar

Idiomas: Español, idiomas indígenas

Moneda: El peso chileno

Población: 15.7 millones

Chile's history includes many important figures. José de San Martín and Bernardo O'Higgins led the fight for independence from Spain. Eduardo Frei Montalva and Salvador Allende were presidents who fought to return industry to Chileans and divide large land holdings **(latifundios).** Augusto Pinochet took control of Chile by force and governed as a dictator for seventeen years.

Chile boasts many famous writers, like Nobel Prize winners Pablo Neruda and Gabriela Mistral, and the contemporary novelist Isabel Allende. Seafood is inexpensive and plentiful in Chile. Some other typical foods are **completo** (a hot dog covered in mayonnaise), **empanadas** (meat pies similar to turnovers), and **aliado** (a ham and cheese sandwich).

¡Léelo en español!

Dos poetas chilenos: Gabriela Mistral y Pablo Neruda La literatura latinoamericana es rica en poesía, cuentos[1] y novelas. Muchos autores ganan premios, incluyendo el estimado Premio Nobel. Gabriela Mistral y Pablo Neruda son dos poetas chilenos que han ganado[2] el Premio Nobel. Son conocidos en todo el mundo.

 Gabriela Mistral (1889–1957) era del pueblo de Vicuña. Era maestra en escuela primaria y directora de una escuela en Punta Arenas que ahora lleva su nombre[3], el Liceo Gabriela Mistral. Ella es una poeta famosa.

 Pablo Neruda (1904–1973) es de la ciudad de Valparaíso. Neruda escribe muchas formas de poesía, como versos sencillos, sonetos de amor, odas a las cosas elementales y poemas políticos. Éste es un ejemplo de su poesía.

**Antes de amarte, amor, nada era mío
vacilé por las calles y las cosas:
nada contaba ni tenía nombre:
el mundo era del aire que esperaba.**

(From *Cien sonetos de amor.*)
In this stanza, the author, Neruda,

[1] short stories [2] have won [3] bears her name

¿Dónde se habla español?

Reading Poetry There are a few things you can do to help you understand poetry. Rewrite a line of poetry so it is a regular sentence. Read the sentences like a story to decipher what the author is telling us. Draw a picture of the scene the author is painting with words. Make a list of any comparisons. Make a list of the feelings the author seems to be expressing.

Recognizing Cognates
What do you think these words mean: **incluyendo, versos, sonetos, odas?** Use these cognates to help you understand what is being said about these Chilean poets.

says that before he fell in love with his wife, he wandered through the streets among objects and nothing had a name or mattered. The world belonged to waiting air.

¡Comprendo!

Draw a picture representing the fragment of poetry. Label in Spanish some of the things mentioned in the fragment.

En la cocina

Objetivos

- To name things you find in the kitchen and say where they are

- To talk about some things you do in the kitchen

- To talk about things you do in general

- To learn about cooking and mealtimes in Spanish-speaking countries

A woman cooks at Libertad Market food stand in Guadalajara, Mexico.

¿Sabías que...?

- In Spanish-speaking countries, some kitchens in the countryside may be very simple. People there may even do their cooking over an open fire. In cities and suburbs, kitchens look more like typical ones in the United States.

- Mexico produces beautiful ceramic tiles **(azulejos)** that are used in kitchens as well as in other rooms. The tiles come in all sizes, colors, and designs. They've become so popular that many people in the United States have kitchens that look **muy mexicanas.**

¿Cómo se dice?

¿Qué usas en la cocina?

—¿Usas mucho el lavaplatos en tu cocina?

—Sí, siempre uso el lavaplatos.

la cocina

el gabinete

el grifo

el fregadero

el refrigerador

la estufa

el horno

el cajón

el lavaplatos

¡Úsalo!

A Compare these two drawings and find six differences between them. Take turns pointing out the differences with a partner.

MODELO —En la cocina A hay dos cajones, y en la cocina B hay tres cajones.

A

B

CONEXIÓN CON LA CULTURA

Lifestyle Many people in Spanish-speaking countries spend more time cooking than people do in the United States. They don't usually buy as many canned or frozen foods as people in the United States do, and they tend to use fresh ingredients. Does your family like to cook from scratch or do they prefer ready-made food? Why?

B Look at the pictures and decide with a partner where these items would be in your own kitchen.

MODELO —¿Dónde está(n)?

—En el refrigerador.

el refrigerador

el gabinete

el lavaplatos

el cajón

el horno

CONEXIÓN CON LAS MATEMÁTICAS

Lines of Symmetry Work with a partner to determine whether these Mexican and Spanish tiles are symmetrical or not. Discuss with your partner where the lines of symmetry should go.

MODELO Tienes que dibujar una línea vertical.

◎ ◎ ◎ **Compara** ◎ ◎ ◎	
En inglés	**En español**
line	la línea
vertical	vertical
horizontal	horizontal
diagonal	diagonal

Entre amigos

Design your dream kitchen! Look through magazines, newspapers, and catalogs for kitchen items that you know. Cut them out and gather them for your kitchen.

Work with two classmates and decide what appliances and furniture you want and where they should go. You'll need to answer questions like these:

¿Cuál te gusta más?
¿Quieres un refrigerador grande o pequeño?
¿Cuántos gabinetes vamos a necesitar?
¿Dónde vamos a poner el lavaplatos?

Place all the items where you want them on a piece of posterboard. This will be your kitchen. Present your poster to the class. Explain what you included and describe where those items are. Make sure that you are not missing anything important in your kitchen.

En resumen

el cajón	la cocina
el fregadero	la estufa
el gabinete	
el grifo	
el horno	
el lavaplatos	
el refrigerador	

¿Cómo se dice?

¿Qué más hay en la cocina?

 —Marta, ¿hay un tostador en la cocina?

—Sí.

—¿Y qué más hay?

—También hay un abrelatas.

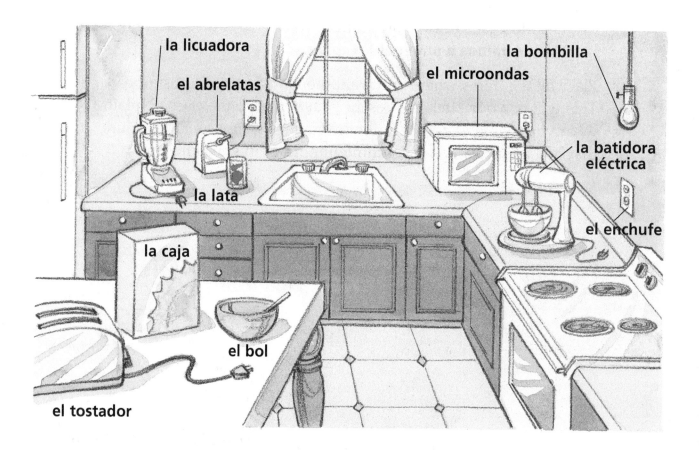

la licuadora

el abrelatas

la lata

la caja

el bol

el tostador

el microondas

la bombilla

la batidora eléctrica

el enchufe

 —Mario, ¿qué usas ahora?

—Uso la batidora eléctrica.

¡Úsalo!

A Work with four or five classmates. Write the names of the kitchen items listed below on pieces of paper. Fold the pieces of paper and drop them into a bag. One player is the "guesser" and leaves the room. Another player draws an item from the bag and reads its name. The "guesser" comes back into the room. The whole group acts out using the item. The "guesser" has to figure out what item is being used.

> **MODELO** —¿Usan el abrelatas?
>
> —Sí, usamos el abrelatas.

| la bombilla | el enchufe | el bol | el tostador | la batidora |
| el microondas | la caja | la lata | la licuadora | eléctrica |

CONEXIÓN CON LAS CIENCIAS

Electricity If you travel to Latin America or Spain, you can't just plug in your blow dryer wherever you go! The power of the current, which is 220 Volts, and the shapes of outlets are not the same as in the United States, which uses 110 Volts. You might burn out your electrical appliances if you plug them into the wrong outlet.

Some items, such as laptop computers, are ready-made to accept several kinds of current. But you need an adapter so you can fit the plug into the outlets. Most items require a current converter—which changes the power of the current—in order to work properly.

Work with a partner and make a list of kitchen items that need to be plugged in to work.

> **MODELO** Necesitamos un enchufe para...

B Get together with a partner. Close your book and ask your partner if certain items are in the kitchen below. Your partner answers according to the picture. As you ask your questions, make two lists: one of what's in the kitchen and one of what's not.

> **MODELO** —¿Hay una licuadora en la cocina?
>
> —No, no hay una licuadora en la cocina.

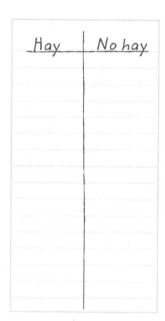

C Get together with a partner. Write the names of twelve different kitchen items on cards. Mix up the cards and distribute them between you. Then each of you draws a kitchen on a sheet of paper. Take turns telling each other where the items on your cards are. Then see if you can draw your partner's kitchen on another sheet of paper. Compare kitchens. Did you put all the items in the right place?

> **MODELO** Los platos están dentro del gabinete.

CONEXIÓN CON LA SALUD

Kitchen Safety Before starting to make *any* recipe, get an adult's permission to work in the kitchen. If your recipe requires using knives, the stove, or electrical kitchen appliances, you should always work with an adult. By having an adult around, you can avoid surprises, stay safe, and still have fun while you cook. Now, with a partner, decide if you will need an adult's help to use the following:

l. usar el microondas

2. usar el tostador

3. usar el grifo

4. usar el horno

5. usar el gabinete

6. usar el cajón

7. usar el fregadero

8. usar el bol

MODELO —¿Necesitas un adulto para usar la batidora eléctrica?

—Sí, necesitas un adulto.

En resumen

el abrelatas	la batidora eléctrica
el bol	la bombilla
el enchufe	la caja
el microondas	la lata
el tostador	la licuadora

Lección 2

ciento treinta y tres 133

¿Cómo se dice?

What do you do in the kitchen?

What's one of the main things you do in the kitchen? You cook, right? The verb that means "to cook" is **cocinar.** Look at these sentences to see how to talk about cooking.

Singular

Yo **cocino** muy bien.

Tú no **cocinas.**

Él siempre **cocina.**

Plural

Nosotras **cocinamos** muy bien.

¿**Cocinan** mucho ustedes?

Ellos **cocinan** muy mal.

What endings do you use when you're talking about yourself and your friends cooking? What endings do you use to talk about two or more people cooking?

Because it ends in **-ar, cocinar** is called an **-ar** verb. You've already used a number of **-ar** verbs before. Now here's a new one: **mirar.** It means "to look at" or "to watch."

El gato **mira** el pájaro.   **Miramos** la televisión.

Almost all **-ar** verbs change in exactly the same way when you use them in sentences:

Yo mir**o**...
Tú mir**as**...
Él / Ella / Usted mir**a**...
Nosotros / Nosotras mir**amos**...
Ellos / Ellas / Ustedes mir**an**...

Another useful **-ar** verb to know is **necesitar.** It means "to need."

Yo necesit**o**...
Tú necesit**as**...
Él / Ella / Usted necesit**a**...
Nosotros / Nosotras necesit**amos**...
Ellos / Ellas / Ustedes necesit**an**...

¡Úsalo!

A Who says these things? Get together with a partner and take turns reading these sentences out loud. Your partner responds by telling you who is doing each thing.

¡Ojo! Some sentences may have more than one correct answer.

Ustedes	Ellas	Nosotros	Yo	Tú	Él

1. Cocinamos una cena grande los domingos.
2. Comen en la cocina.
3. Miro la televisión en la sala de estar.
4. Pintas las paredes de la casa.
5. Necesita una alfombra verde.
6. Llevan suéteres amarillos.

B Get together with a partner and look at this picture. Choose someone in the picture, but don't tell your partner who it is. Describe what the person or animal is doing. Your partner has to guess whom you chose. Take turns choosing and guessing.

Partner A: Say something about the person or animal you chose.

Partner B: Point at the correct person or animal.

> MODELO —Necesita unos zapatos.
> —¿Es ella?

C Make a chart like this one and conduct a survey about home life. Get together with a group of five or six classmates. Find out whose family members cook a lot, whether they use a computer, whether they watch TV on weekends, and what new clothes they might need.

Ask these questions and add others of your own.

	Sí	No
¿Tus padres cocinan mucho?	Gabriela, Juan	
¿Usas la computadora en casa?		
¿Miras la televisión los fines de semana?		
¿Necesitas ropa nueva? ¿Qué necesitas?		

Then, each member of your group tells the rest of the class something about the people in your group.

MODELO —Los padres de Gabriela y Juan cocinan mucho. Margarita mira la televisión los fines de semana. Mira el programa...

CONEXIÓN CON LA CULTURA

Making Gazpacho Look at these pictures. They show how to make a typical Spanish dish: **gazpacho.** It's a tomato-based soup served cold.

Get together with a partner. Make a list of the kitchen items needed to prepare and serve this dish. See who can come up with the most items.

Entre amigos

Get together with a partner and write on different cards all the kitchen items you have learned. Put your cards in a box with those of the rest of the class. Choose one of the dishes below and take five cards from the box. Keep the ones you need to prepare your dish. Find the people who have the other items that you need. When giving items to each other, you can say **Toma.** ("Here you go.")

—¿Tienes un tostador?

—Sí.

—¿Necesitas el tostador?

—No, no necesito el tostador. Toma.

En resumen

	cocinar	mirar	necesitar	endings
	cocin-	mir-	necesit-	
(Yo)	cocino	miro	necesito	-o
(Tú)	cocinas	miras	necesitas	-as
(Él, Ella, Ud.)	cocina	mira	necesita	-a
(Nosotros, Nosotras)	cocinamos	miramos	necesitamos	-amos
(Ellos, Ellas, Uds.)	cocinan	miran	necesitan	-an

¿Cómo se dice?

What else do you do in the kitchen?

What do you do after you've cooked something? You eat it, of course! Study these sentences to learn how to talk about eating.

Singular

Yo **como** en la cocina.

¡Tú **comes** mucho!

Ella **come** poco.

Plural

Nosotros **comemos** en el comedor.

¡Ustedes **comen** bien!

Ellos siempre **comen** mucho.

The verb **comer,** which means "to eat," is an **-er** verb. Most **-er** verbs have exactly the same endings.

Take the word **correr,** for example. It means "to run."

Yo corr**o** en el parque.
Tú no corr**es** hoy.
Ella corr**e** en el gimnasio.

Nosotras corr**emos** mucho.
Ellos corr**en** a la escuela.
Ustedes corr**en** bien.

Did you notice that the endings were exactly the same as the endings for the different sentences using **comer?** It's the same for **aprender, comprender, leer,** and most of the other **-er** verbs you use.

You've already learned the word for "can opener." Here's the verb that means "to open"—**abrir.**

Singular

Abro la puerta.

¿**Abres** la puerta del garaje, papá?

Él **abre** la puerta del refrigerador.

Plural

Nosotras **abrimos** la puerta.

Ustedes **abren** las puertas de los gabinetes.

Ellas **abren** la puerta del salón de clase.

If you know the endings to use with **abrir,** you know what to use with most **-ir** verbs. This is true for **-ir** verbs you already know, such as **escribir,** as well as those you haven't studied yet, such as **vivir** (which means "to live") and **batir** ("to beat or to whip," as with **la batidora).**

CONEXIÓN CON LA CULTURA

Mealtimes Mealtimes in Spanish-speaking countries are important. It's when the entire family spends time together. In some countries there may be several courses, such appetizers or fruit first, then a main course with meat or fish, and salad and dessert afterward. It's common for Spanish speakers to stay at the table for a while. This is called **la sobremesa.** People can sit around the table talking for a long time—especially on weekends and holidays!

¡Úsalo!

A Get together with a partner and ask about his or her activities. Fill out a chart like this one.

> **MODELO** —¿Cantas mucho o poco?
>
> —Canto poco.
> *or* **Nunca canto.**

Now get together with another pair and ask them the same questions, addressed to both of them. They take turns answering according to what they wrote in their charts.

	mucho	poco	nunca
cantar		X	
correr			
practicar deportes			
estudiar			
aprender			
leer			
escribir			
cocinar			

> **MODELO** —¿Ustedes corren mucho?
>
> —Yo corro mucho, pero él (ella) corre poco.

B What do you do in different situations? With a partner, take turns thinking of a complete answer to each question.

> **MODELO** Hace mucho calor en tu dormitorio. ¿Qué haces?
>
> —Abro la ventana.

1. Hay un lápiz y un cuaderno en tu pupitre. ¿Qué haces?
2. Hace mucho frío. Vas a ir a la escuela. ¿Qué haces?
3. Hay una lata en la mesa. Tú vas a cocinar. ¿Qué haces?
4. Quieres aprender español muy bien. ¿Qué haces?
5. Estás en el comedor. Tienes un plato de comida delante. ¿Qué haces?

C Guess who does what! With a partner, read the phrases and match each one to one or more of the people below. Then write sentences about what they do. **¡Ojo!** The same person may do different things, and two or three different people may do the same thing! Take turns reading your sentences to your partner.

José

Sra. Pérez, Juan y Marta

Sr. Casas

MODELO llevar vestido

—Marta, la hija de la señora Pérez, lleva vestido.

1. ir a la escuela todos los días
2. tener hambre por la tarde
3. mirar la televisión los sábados
4. escribir en la computadora
5. leer libros por la tarde
6. gustarle los animales
7. cocinar todos los días
8. no gustarle los niños impacientes

Entre amigos

Read the letter Sara from Honduras wrote to her new key pal.

De: Sara Hurtado [sarahurtado@hurtadomail.com]
Para: Ti
Asunto: Mi vida en Honduras
Fecha: miércoles, 15 de septiembre

Querido(a) amigo(a):

Me llamo Sara Hurtado. Me gusta practicar deportes con mi familia. Todos los domingos corremos o caminamos. Y los sábados patino con mi papá. ¿Practican ustedes deportes? ¿Nadan mucho tus hermanos?

Tengo amigos en muchos países y les escribo muchos e-mails. ¿Escribes tú e-mails?

En las noches a mi familia y a mí nos gusta mirar la televisión en la sala de estar. Mi programa favorito es "Espacio 2010." ¿Miran ustedes la televisión? ¿Cuál es tu programa favorito?

¡Hasta luego!
Sara

Now get together with a partner and write a letter to Sara. Be sure to answer her questions.

En resumen

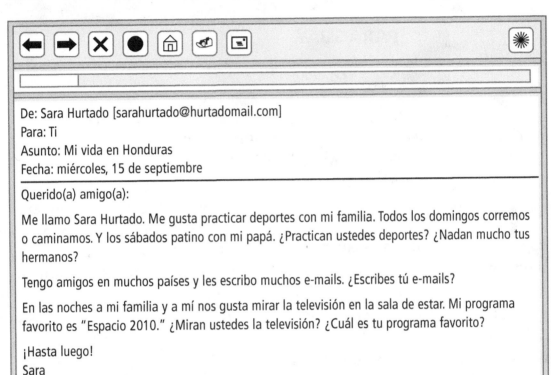

	-ar cocinar	-er aprender	-ir abrir
(Yo)	cocino	aprendo	abro
(Tú)	cocinas	aprendes	abres
(Él, Ella, Ud.)	cocina	aprende	abre
(Nosotros, Nosotras)	cocinamos	aprendemos	abrimos
(Ellos, Ellas, Uds.)	cocinan	aprenden	abren

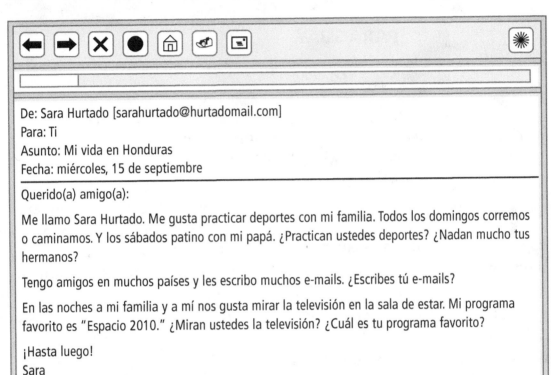

¿Dónde se habla español?

PARAGUAY

Asunción

Paraguay

Paraguay is one of the two land-locked countries in South America. It is about the size of California, and it is surrounded by Bolivia, Brazil, and Argentina. The Paraguay River divides the country into two regions. To the east there are many national parks and preserves in the grasslands and forests. In these parks and preserves you can see many types of wildlife. There are reptiles like the anaconda and the cayman, and birds, including storks. To the west there is an extensive plain known as the **Gran Chaco,** where the main industry is cattle farming.

Paraguay's main products are beef, maize, sugarcane, lumber, cotton, and soybeans. Movies, theater, and dancing are popular forms of entertainment. **Cachaca** is a popular tropical beat that can be heard in Paraguay's clubs along with all types of music, including jazz. In one traditional dance, **la danza de la botella,** people dance with bottles on their heads.

Popular souvenirs are traditional lace made by hand (**ñandutí),** carved wooden animals, hammocks, leather goods, and handmade guitars. Popular foods include grilled meats (**parrillada), mandioca, chipas** and **empanadas.** Soccer is the most popular sport.

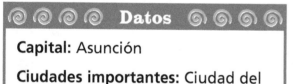

Datos

Capital: Asunción

Ciudades importantes: Ciudad del Este, Encarnación, Juan Pedro Caballero, Concepción, Villarrica

Idiomas: Español, guaraní

Moneda: El guaraní

Población: 6 millones

¡Léelo en español!

Los guaraníes: ayer y hoy Los guaraníes son los indígenas de Paraguay. Los guaraníes vivían[1] en Paraguay cuando llegaron los españoles en el siglo XVI. Los guaraníes fueron muy simpáticos con los españoles. Los españoles se casaron con[2] los guaraníes. Los españoles adoptaron comidas, palabras y otras costumbres de los guaraníes. Los misionarios, jesuitas trajeron cultura y agricultura a los guaraníes.

Hoy día[3] en Paraguay la influencia de los guaraníes todavía es muy fuerte. Hay más de seis millones de personas en Paraguay, y más de setenta y cinco por ciento[4] son mestizos de ascendencia española y guaraní. El español es el idioma principal del país, pero Paraguay es bilingüe. El guaraní es el otro idioma del país. Palabras del guaraní se mezclan[5] con el español.

El dinero de Paraguay se llama el guaraní. Mucha comida refleja[6] la influencia guaraní también.

[1] lived   [2] married   [3] Nowadays   [4] percent
[5] mix   [6] reflects

Reading Strategy

Using the Title Look at the title of the reading. Titles will help you understand what the reading or poem is about. Keep the title in mind as you read. The title also tells you the main idea and what the author thinks is most important.

Recognizing Cognates What do you think these words mean: **adoptaron, bilingüe?** Use these cognates to help you understand what is being said about the people of Paraguay.

¡Comprendo!

Answer in English.

1. Describe the relationship between the Spaniards and the Guaraní.

2. What did the Jesuit missionaries do for the Guaraní?

3. How many people today are of mixed blood (**mestizos**)?

4. What is the influence of the Guaraní today in the language and money of Paraguay?

Vamos a limpiar

Objetivos

- To talk about household chores
- To talk about having to do something
- To discuss things you've just finished doing
- To learn about housekeeping in Spanish-speaking countries

Laundry is hung to dry on a fence overlooking the city of Merida, Venezuela.

A boy helps his parents with the household chores.

A beautiful tile floor in the corridor of a Santo Domingo, Dominican Republic home

¿Sabías que...?

In Spanish-speaking countries:

- Many people hang their laundry outside to dry, even if they have a dryer. They like the nice smell that fresh air gives their clothes.

- It's common for families to have a cleaning person come into their homes. Sometimes the person even lives with the family.

- Wall-to-wall carpeting isn't as popular as it is in the United States. Many people are proud of their home's beautiful wood or tile floors, and they don't want to cover them with carpeting. Bare floors are cooler in places where it gets hot. People do use area rugs, however.

¿Cómo se dice?

¿Vamos a limpiar la casa?

 —Vamos a limpiar la casa, ¿verdad, mamá?

—Sí. Primero, tú vas a sacar la basura. Yo voy a quitar el polvo.

los quehaceres

barrer el piso

pasar la aspiradora

limpiar el piso

quitar el polvo

regar las plantas

sacar la basura

—¿Con qué vas a limpiar el piso?
—Con el trapeador.

la escoba

la aspiradora

el trapeador

el trapo

—¿Limpias el piso sin la escoba?
—Sí, uso la aspiradora.

¿Sabías que...?

It's common for Spanish speakers in different countries to have different names for household items. For example, there are many different words for **trapeador.** Some people may call it **el estropajo, la mopa, el mocho,** or **la fregona,** among other names.

¡Úsalo!

A Today is Saturday and Jorge is getting ready to clean up his room. Get together with a partner. Take turns saying the chores that you think Jorge will do.

> **MODELO** —Va a barrer el piso.

B With a partner, draw a large floor plan of a house on butcher paper. Label all the rooms. In each room, list all the chores you might be able to do there. You can list the same chore in different rooms. Use the Spanish you know to find new ways to name the chores! Here's an example:

> **MODELO** Limpiar mi ropero.

Compare your lists with those of other pairs. Who thought of the most chores? Which room has the most chores of all?

Entre amigos

Play a matching game! Get together with a partner. Make two sets of cards. One set has household chores on them. The other one has names of objects and appliances used to do those chores. Put the cards facedown in two piles.

Now, pick a card from the pile of household chores and ask questions based on the card. For example, if your card is **limpiar el piso,** you can ask: **¿Con qué vas a limpiar el piso?** Your partner picks a card from the other pile and answers according to what's on it, such as: **Con el lavaplatos.** Since that's not right, both cards go to the bottom of the pile!

If your partner matches a chore with the correct appliance, he or she gets to keep the chore card. The other card is returned to its pile, since it might be used for more than one chore!

CONEXIÓN CON LA SALUD

Allergies and Asthma To prevent dust allergies and asthma, it's important to keep the house clean and well-ventilated. With a partner, think of all the chores you should do to help prevent allergies and asthma in your home, for example: **pasar la aspiradora.**

En resumen

los quehaceres	pasar la aspiradora	el trapeador
barrer el piso	quitar el polvo	el trapo
limpiar el piso	regar las plantas	la aspiradora
limpiar la casa	sacar la basura	la escoba

¿Cómo se dice?

¿Qué haces en la casa?

 —Papá, ¿qué haces ahora?

—Tengo que lavar la ropa. Tengo que secar la ropa también.

recoger las cosas

lavar la ropa

secar la ropa

colgar la ropa

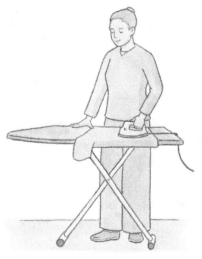

planchar la ropa

—Mamá, ¿está limpio mi suéter?

—Sí. Está cerca de la secadora.

la lavadora

la secadora

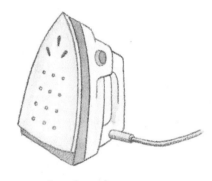

la plancha

Está sucio.

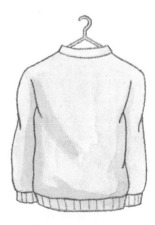

Está limpio.

 ## CONEXIÓN CON LOS ESTUDIOS SOCIALES

Trade Did you know that many household electric appliances sold in the United States, including vacuum cleaners, washers, and dryers, are assembled in Mexican factories? Mexico, in turn, imports oil and farming equipment from the United States.

¡Úsalo!

A Your family has asked you to help more around the house. You have to do a chore every day. Use a chart like this one to show when you will do one thing each day and the place where you will do it. Then get together with a partner. Ask each other questions to find out what the other one will do each day.

MODELO —¿Qué haces los lunes?

—Los lunes barro el piso de la cocina.

	lunes	martes	miércoles	jueves	viernes	sábado	domingo
	X la cocina						

B This house sure needs a good cleaning! Get together with a partner and describe what you see here. Your partner tells you what he or she will do about it.

MODELO —Hay mucha ropa en el piso.

—Voy a colgar la ropa en el ropero.

 Entre amigos

Work with a partner. Together, think of one chore that you have decided to do at home or at school. For example: **Vamos a limpiar las ventanas en la escuela.**

Now get together with another pair. They have to guess what chore you chose!

—¿**Van a lavar la ropa en la casa?**

—**No.** *or* **Sí.**

En resumen

Voy a colgar la ropa.
        lavar
        planchar
        secar
        recoger las cosas.

la lavadora
la plancha
la secadora

Está limpio.
      sucio.

Lección 2

ciento cincuenta y cinco **155**

¿Cómo se dice?

Talking about what you have to do

What words do you use to talk about having to do something? Look at these sentences and see.

Singular	**Plural**

Tengo que lavar la ropa.

Tenemos que quitar el polvo.

Tienes que colgar tu ropa.

Ustedes **tienen que** limpiar el piso.

Ella **tiene que** regar las plantas.

Ellos **tienen que** sacar la basura.

When you talk about things you have to do, you use a form of **tener + que +** *the action verb.*

¡Úsalo!

A What does your family need to do? Get together with a partner, who will play your mom or dad. Read each sentence to your partner. Your partner tells you what the family (**nosotros**) needs to do.

> **MODELO** —Hay mucha basura en la cocina.
>
> —Tenemos que sacar la basura.
>
> —El piso de la cocina está limpio.
>
> —No tenemos que limpiar el piso de la cocina.

1. Mi ropa está muy sucia.
2. La alfombra de la sala de estar está muy sucia.
3. Las alfombras de los dormitorios están limpias.
4. Hay mucho polvo en los estantes.
5. Hay muchas cosas en los muebles.
6. No hay mucho polvo en el tocador.
7. La ropa limpia de mis hermanos está en las camas.
8. Hay muchas cosas en el piso de mi dormitorio.

CONEXIÓN CON LOS ESTUDIOS SOCIALES

Clean Up the World Clean Up the World (**A limpiar el mundo**) is a worldwide cleanup campaign sponsored by the United Nations and by private companies. It has many participants all over Latin America. On the third weekend in September, people in every town, neighborhood, and city get together to clean up a beach, a river, a school, or a park. They also come up with ideas to improve their local environment. What cleanup efforts are there where you live?

B You have so many chores you had to make a schedule like the one below. Get together with a partner. Your partner closes his or her book and asks you questions about your schedule. Then he or she writes one based on your answers. Are they the same?

Partner A: Ask if and when your partner has to do each chore.

Partner B: Answer the questions based on the schedule.

> MODELO —¿Tienes que barrer el piso?
>
> —Sí.
>
> —¿Cuándo tienes que barrer el piso?
>
> —Tengo que barrer el piso los lunes.

lunes	martes	miércoles	jueves	viernes	sábado	domingo
barrer el piso	sacar la basura	pasar la aspiradora	recoger la ropa sucia	lavar y secar la ropa	planchar la ropa	limpiar el piso

C Think of all the things you would have to do in your room for it to be totally clean and tidy. Get together with a partner and tell each other about your rooms. Whose room is messier?

> MODELO —Tengo que lavar la ropa, pasar la aspiradora...

CONEXIÓN CON LAS MATEMÁTICAS

Time Andrew is very busy today. He has to wash and dry three loads of laundry. It's noon right now. The washing machine takes 45 minutes to wash a load, and the dryer takes an hour to dry it. When will he finish doing the laundry?

CONEXIÓN CON LA SALUD

Household Chores Write down the chores that each member of your family has to do. Consider all the chores that you have learned. Write them down.

> **Mamá tiene que...**
>
> **Papá tiene que...**
>
> **Yo tengo que...**
>
> **Mis hermanos/as tienen que...**
>
> **Todos** (*All of us*) **tenemos que...**

Now get together with a partner and compare the chores. Are they similar?

Decide whether the chores in your family are equally divided among all the members. Do you think you should do more to help around the house?

En resumen

(Yo)	**tengo**		lavar la ropa.
(Tú)	**tienes**		quitar el polvo.
(Él, Ella, Ud.)	**tiene**	**que**	colgar la ropa.
(Nosotros, Nosotras)	**tenemos**		limpiar el piso.
(Ellos, Ellas, Uds.)	**tienen**		sacar la basura.

¿Cómo se dice?

What have you just finished doing?

Look at these pictures and sentences.

Tengo que regar las plantas.

Acabo de regar las plantas.

Tenemos que recoger las cosas.

Acabamos de recoger las cosas.

You've learned how to use **tener que** + *an action verb* to talk about what you have to do. Now compare the pictures and sentences on the left with those on the right. What do you think the sentences on the right are about?

The verb **acabar + de** + *a verb* lets you talk about what you have just finished doing.

¡Úsalo!

A Parents are always telling you what to do, and sometimes you've already done it! Get together with a partner and play the roles of a parent and a child. The parent tells the child what to do—but the child has just finished doing it!

Partner A: Tell your partner a chore he or she has to do.

Partner B: Say you've already done it!

> MODELO —Tienes que colgar la ropa.
>
> —Acabo de colgar la ropa.

B You and your partner have to clean the house. Your partner is checking to see which chores are done and which aren't. He or she makes comments, and you say that you just did it, or that you need to do it, according to what your partner says.

Partner A: Read each comment you see here.

Partner B: Say that you have just done it or that you still need to do it.

> MODELO —El piso de la cocina está limpio.
>
> —Sí, acabo de barrer el piso.
>
> —El piso del cuarto de baño está sucio.
>
> —Sí, tengo que barrer el piso.

1. Hay mucho polvo en los muebles.
2. La ropa no está en el ropero.
3. La ropa en el piso está sucia.
4. La alfombra de la sala de estar está sucia.
5. La ropa en mi ropero está limpia.
6. No hay basura en la cocina.
7. Las alfombras de los dormitorios están sucias.
8. No hay polvo en el comedor.

C Look at the "before" and "after" pictures of the Molinero kitchen.

| Antes | Después |

Get together with a partner. One of you takes the **Antes** picture of the Molinero kitchen and writes as many sentences as you can that indicate what the Molinero family has to do—for example:

MODELO **Tienen que usar el lavaplatos.**

The other partner takes the **Después** picture of the Molinero kitchen and writes as many sentences as possible that indicate what they have just done to clean it up—for example:

MODELO **Acaban de barrer el piso.**

When you and your partner have finished, compare your sentences. How many chores did you both write about? Compare your sentences with those of other pairs. Which pair of students came up with the most ideas?

D Get together with a partner. Make a list of five things for another pair to do. Now get together with another pair. Tell them what they have to do, and they have to pretend to do it for ten seconds. Then they tell you when they're done!

MODELO —¿Qué tenemos que hacer?

—Tienen que lavar la ropa.

(Pretend to wash clothes for ten seconds.)

—Acabamos de lavar la ropa.

After the other pair does your five tasks, they get to assign tasks to you!

CONEXIÓN CON LAS MATEMÁTICAS

Making Schedules What chores do you do at home? Make your own schedule of chores with dates and times for this week. Then get together with three or four classmates. Show your schedule to them and tell them about it. Answer any questions they have. Ask them about their schedules. What do they have to do? When do they have to do it? Where? What have they just done yesterday or today? Write down what they tell you.

When you've finished, talk about chores with the class. Who has the most chores? Who has the fewest?

En resumen

(Yo)	**acabo**		
(Tú)	**acabas**		
(Él, Ella, Ud.)	**acaba**	**de**	regar las plantas.
(Nosotros, Nosotras)	**acabamos**		recoger las cosas.
(Ellos, Ellas, Uds.)	**acaban**		

¿Dónde se habla español?

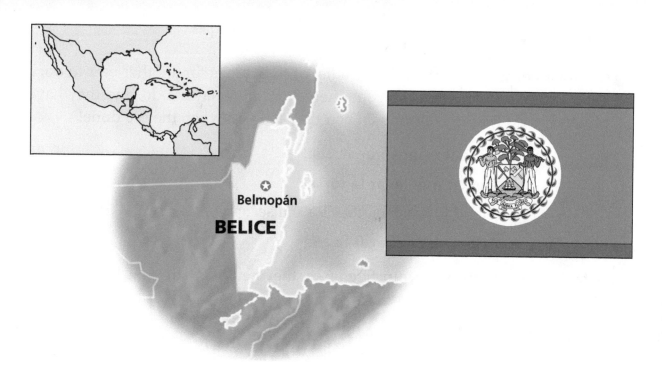

Belmopán

BELICE

Belice

Belize is a small country that borders Mexico and Guatemala on the west, while the Caribbean Sea stretches along its eastern border.
It is about the size of the state of New Jersey, and its people are very friendly and relaxed. Belize was originally claimed by Spain, but the British took over the country later and called it British Honduras.

Even though the country is small, it has many attractions for visitors. There are Mayan ruins to explore. You can hike in beautiful national parks where you will see many birds, like hummingbirds, toucans, and woodpeckers. You might also see a a tapir (shown on the next page), a jaguar, or a howler monkey. If you like sports you can also snorkel around a great barrier reef.

Belize, although small, is a country full of natural wonders.

> ◎◎◎◎ **Datos** ◎◎◎◎
>
> **Capital:** Belmopán
>
> **Ciudades importantes:** Ciudad de Belice, Corozal, Orange Walk, San Pedro (Cayo Ambergris), Dangringa
>
> **Idiomas:** Inglés, inglés criollo, español, maya
>
> **Moneda:** El dólar de belice
>
> **Población:** 266,000

Mayan ruins at Lamanai

¡Léelo en español!

Aventuras en Belice ¿Te gusta bucear[1]? Hay muchas islas pequeñas cerca de Belice donde puedes bucear. Muchas personas pasean en barco para visitar las islas que se llaman "Cayos." Si vas en un barco de Hicaco (Cayo Caulker), puedes ir al arrecife[2] para bucear. Allí puedes ver muchos peces tropicales y unas langostas[3] y manatíes. Es divertido ver los peces de muchos colores y muchos tamaños[4].

Si prefieres viajar en un río, puedes tomar un barco por el río *New River*, de la ciudad de *Orange Walk* a las ruinas de los mayas en Lamanai. En Lamanai, puedes explorar un templo y ver el lugar donde los mayas jugaban[5] su juego de pelota.

[1] scuba dive or snorkel   [2] reef   [3] lobsters
[4] sizes   [5] used to play

Reading Strategy

Using Visuals Pictures tell a story. Look at the pictures and guess what adventures will be described in the reading. What might you see when you snorkel? What might you see when you visit the Mayan ruins?

Recognizing Cognates What do you think these words mean: **tropicales, manatíes, templo?** Use these cognates to help you understand what is being said about Belize.

¡Comprendo!

Answer in English.

1. What are the small islands near the Belizean coast called?

2. How do you get to the barrier reef?

3. Why is the town of Lamanai important?

4. Why is English spoken in Belize?

Un plato de frutas

Objetivos

- To name things you use at the table
- To name different kinds of fruit
- To learn how to talk about putting and bringing things someplace
- To talk about where things are
- To learn about some fruits found in Latin America

A Puerto Rican fruit market

Locals shop at a produce market on Calle Ocho in San José, Costa Rica.

¿Sabías que...?

- Almost all of the bananas you eat are shipped from Latin America.

- Tropical Latin America has many fruits that are not as common in the United States, such as **mangos** and **guayabas** (*guavas*).

- In Paraguay, Uruguay, and Argentina, **mate** is a very popular drink. It's similar to tea, prepared from dried **mate** leaves. You drink it from a special container, with a metal straw.

¿Cómo se dice?

¿Qué hay en la mesa?

 —¿Dónde está el cuchillo?

—Está en la mesa, cerca del plato.

el vaso

el azúcar

la crema

el cuchillo

la servilleta

el tenedor

el plato

el mantel

—¿Qué tienes que hacer ahora?

—¡Ay! Tengo que poner la sal en la mesa.

el platillo

la taza

la sal

la pimienta

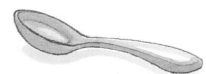

la cuchara

la cucharita

 —¿Necesitas algo?

—Sí, pásame la sal, por favor.

CONEXIÓN CON EL ARTE

Traditional Crafts Different types of traditional weaving and embroidery can be found all over the Spanish-speaking world. **Bolillo** lace is made by hand and treasured for generations. Mothers and grandmothers often give their own **bolillo** tablecloths and other pieces to their daughters and granddaughters as special gifts. What things are passed from one generation to another in your family?

¡Úsalo!

A Your grandparents are coming over for dinner tonight. There will be four people: your grandparents, your mother, and yourself—but the table is not set yet! Some things are missing. Read these sentences to a partner, who tells you if they're true (**verdadero**) or false (**falso**), according to the picture.

> **MODELO** —Tienes que poner el azúcar.
>
> —Falso. No tengo que poner el azúcar.

1. Tienes que poner la pimienta.
2. Tienes que poner la crema.
3. Tienes que poner los cuchillos.
4. Tienes que poner el mantel.
5. Tienes que poner los platos.
6. Tienes que poner los tenedores.

B Get together with a partner and draw on cards twelve items that go on a dining room table. You're going to play against another pair. Sit at a desk with the cards faceup. Tell your partner to pass you something. He or she passes it and tells you to pass something else. The other team does the same at another desk. The team that can pass more things correctly in 30 seconds wins!

> **MODELO** —Pásame un plato.

¿Sabías que...?

Coffee is an important part of the culture in Spanish-speaking countries. It can be served black and strong or with a bit of milk in very small cups, or it can be served with a lot of milk (**café con leche**) in large cups for breakfast, so people can dunk cookies, crackers, or bread in it!

C Draw a kitchen cabinet. Draw some things inside the cabinet and some things outside. Then get together with a partner. Describe what you have in your drawing, but don't show it. See if your partner can come up with a similar drawing!

MODELO —**Hay unos platos fuera del gabinete.**

 ## CONEXIÓN CON LAS MATEMÁTICAS

Changing Units You need to get tablecloths for these tables. For a good fit, a tablecloth should be at least a foot longer and wider than the table on each side.

But the table measurements you have are in centimeters! Find which tablecloth fits each table. Then tell your partner which tablecloth you will put on each table. Remember that 1 inch = 2.54 cm. Show your work.

MODELO —**¿Qué mantel tenemos que poner en la mesa amarilla?**
—**Tenemos que poner el mantel rojo.**

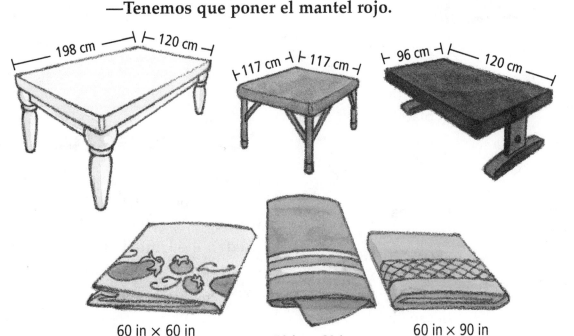

198 cm × 120 cm

117 cm × 117 cm

96 cm × 120 cm

60 in × 60 in

50 in × 60 in

60 in × 90 in

Entre amigos

You and your classmates are going to set a table.

Your teacher will put the different items you need for setting a table into a bag. One student starts by taking out an object. The student puts it inside a box on a table in the front of the room, while the rest of the class covers their eyes so they can't see it.

Then the student pantomimes using the object. The class tries to guess what it is by asking questions about the item:

¿Hay un tenedor en la mesa?

The student who guesses correctly gets to pick the next item from the bag.

En resumen

Tengo que poner	el azúcar	en la mesa.
	el cuchillo	
	el mantel	
	el platillo	
	el plato	
	el tenedor	
	el vaso	
Pásame	la crema.	
	la cuchara.	
	la cucharita.	
	la pimienta.	
	la sal.	
	la servilleta.	
	la taza.	

¿Sabías que...?

Almost all countries in the world use the metric system. Instead of the pounds, gallons, feet, and miles used in the United States, people in other countries use kilograms, liters, meters, and kilometers.

¿Cómo se dice?

¿Te gustan las frutas?

—¿Te gustan las frutas?

—Por supuesto. Me gustan las manzanas y las uvas.

la manzana la pera el durazno

las cerezas las uvas la piña

—¿Qué fruta traes de la tienda?

—Naranjas. ¿Te gustan las naranjas?

las fresas

el plátano

la naranja

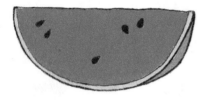

la sandía

el limón

CONEXIÓN CON LA CULTURA

Plantains Not all bananas are sweet. In the Caribbean, there are large green bananas (*plantains*) that are not as sweet as the bananas you eat. They can be prepared in different ways—fried, mashed with garlic, even made into a "lasagna" with plantain strips instead of pasta! You can have them as plantain chips or even in syrup, for dessert. Have *you* ever seen plantains at your local supermarket?

¡Úsalo!

A Imagine that your partner went to the store and brought back one of these baskets. Ask your partner what he or she brought. Your partner secretly picks one of the baskets pictured and tells you the fruits in it. You guess which basket your partner is talking about.

1.

2.

3.

4.

5.

6.

MODELO —¿Qué fruta traes de la tienda?

—Manzanas, limones, plátanos...

—¿Es el número tres?

B Choose three fruits and draw them on a sheet of paper. Think of clues you can use to describe them to your partner.

Partner A: Give your partner a clue about the type of fruit you've chosen.

Partner B: Guess the fruit based on the description.

MODELO —Es mediana y roja.

—La manzana es mediana y roja. ¿Es una manzana?

CONEXIÓN CON LAS MATEMÁTICAS

Multiplying You need to go to the supermarket to buy some fruit. Here's your shopping list. How much money will you need? (Note that **libra** and **lb** mean "pound.") Check your answer with a partner.

$1.89/lb $1.50/lb $3.98/lb $0.89/lb $1.25/lb $1.16/lb $1.40/lb

naranjas
$(3\frac{1}{4}$ libras$)$
cerezas
$(1\frac{1}{4}$ libra$)$
duraznos
$(3$ libras$)$
fresas
$(\frac{1}{2}$ libra$)$
peras
$(1$ libra$)$

En resumen

¿Qué fruta traes de la tienda?

los duraznos   las cerezas
los limones   las fresas
los plátanos   las manzanas
               las naranjas
               las peras
               las piñas
               las sandías
               las uvas

¿Cómo se dice?

Talking about putting and bringing

You've already had some practice with the verb **poner,** which means "to put" or "to place." Look at the picture and the sentences to see how to use **poner.**

1. Yo **pongo** el mantel en la mesa.

2. ¿**Pones** los platos en las sillas?

3. Pepe **pone** los vasos en una mesa.

4. Nosotras **ponemos** las frutas en los platos.

5. Ellos **ponen** una mesa cerca del árbol.

Is **poner** exactly like the other **-er** verbs you know? Do you notice any form of it that's different?

Poner is like the other **-er** verbs, except when you talk about yourself. Then, the ending changes to **-go (pongo).** For that reason, you call **poner** an "irregular verb."

Another irregular **-er** verb that is different only in the **yo** form is **traer,** which means "to bring."

—Yo **traigo** una pera a la escuela.

Did you notice that you have to add an **-i** before the **-go** ending? Like **poner, traer** is the same as the regular **-er** verbs when talking to or about other people:

—¿Qué **traes** tú a la fiesta?
—**Traigo** manzanas y fresas.

—¿Qué **trae** Luisa?
—**Trae** las servilletas.

—¿Qué **traen** ustedes?
—**Traemos** una sandía grande.

—¿Qué **traen** Ana y Carlos?
—**Traen** los platos y vasos.

¿Sabías que...?

Use **poner** to say "set the table."
Pongo la mesa means "I'm setting the table." or "I set the table."

¡Úsalo!

A Tell your partner different things that you bring to school in your backpack. Think of real things and silly things you would not bring. Your partner guesses if what you're saying is true (**verdadero**) or false (**falso**).

> **MODELO** —Traigo un escritorio a la escuela.
>
> —¡Falso!

 CONEXIÓN CON EL ARTE

Still Life Look at these paintings. They are called "still lifes" because nothing in them can move around on its own. Describe to a partner the things you see in them.

"Watermelon"
Isy Ochoa

"Still Life: Basket of Peaches"
Raphaelle Peale

Your teacher will bring some fruit and utensils to class. Work with a partner to arrange them on a table so that you can draw your own still life. Take turns telling each other what you're putting on the table.

> **MODELO** Pongo los plátanos en el plato.

B Everyone's getting ready for a big party! Get together with a partner. Choose one of these pictures and cover the other one with a piece of paper. Your partner will do the same with the other picture. Tell each other who is doing what and find four differences between the two pictures.

Partner A: Ask your partner what each person is putting on the table, according to your picture.

Partner B: Answer according to your picture.

> **MODELO** —¿Ana pone las manzanas en la mesa?
>
> —No, Ana pone las servilletas en la mesa.

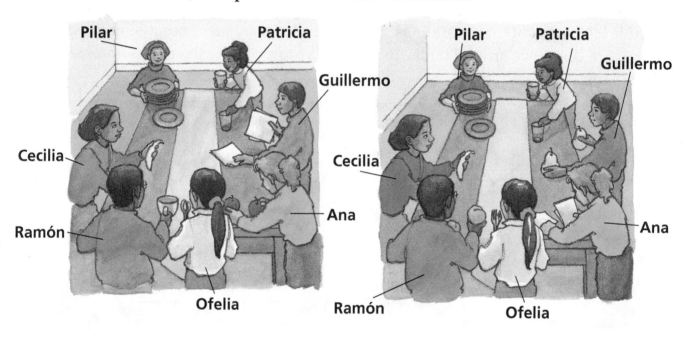

C Here's a list of things you need for a picnic. On a card, write one thing you're bringing.

Sit in a circle with four or five classmates. One person starts by saying what he or she is bringing, based on the card. The person to the right promises to put it on the picnic table. Go around the circle until everyone has said what he or she will bring.

servilletas
platos
cucharas
tenedores
cuchillos
vasos
fruta
estéreo / música
un mantel
una mesa
azúcar

MODELO —Traigo las servilletas.

—Pongo las servilletas en la mesa. Traigo los platos.

Keep track of the items. At the end, each person mentions something on the list that no one is bringing, and that all of you (**nosotros**) have to buy.

MODELO —Tenemos que comprar un mantel.

CONEXIÓN CON LAS MATEMÁTICAS

Division and Remainder You need to set a table for twenty-five guests, but you don't have enough dinnerware! This is what you have: 5 glasses, 8 forks, 7 knives, 13 plates, 12 soup spoons, and 10 teaspoons.

You need to complete each table setting as shown here. You go to the store and see that these items are sold in packages.

- glasses in 6-count packages
- mixed forks, knives, and soup spoons in 12-count packages
- teaspoons in 24-count packages
- napkins in 15-count packages
- plates in 6-count packages

Find out how many packages of each item you have to buy. How many leftover pieces will you have?

En resumen

	poner	traer
(Yo)	pongo	traigo
(Tú)	pones	traes
(Él, Ella, Ud.)	pone	trae
(Nosotros, Nosotras)	ponemos	traemos
(Ellos, Ellas, Uds.)	ponen	traen

¿Cómo se dice?

Describing where things are located

How do you say that something is on top of something else? How do you say that something is under something else? Look at these pictures and sentences to learn how.

La sandía está **sobre** la mesa.

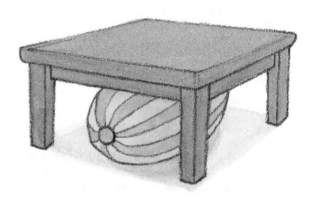

La sandía está **debajo de** la mesa.

Juan pone el vaso **sobre** el televisor.

Ahora pone el vaso **debajo del** televisor.

Use **sobre** to talk about things that are "on top of" or "on" other things. Remember that you can also use **en** to say that something is "on" another thing.

Use **debajo de** to talk about things that are "under" or "underneath" other things. Remember, when **de** comes before **el,** the words combine to form **del.**

¡Úsalo!

A Your three wild cousins have just left after a week-long visit. The house is upside down! Look at the pictures, then use **sobre** or **debajo de** to tell a partner where everything is. Take turns.

> **MODELO** —**Los platos están debajo de la cama.**

1.

2.

3.

4.

5.

6.

7.

8.

9.

B Look around the room for an object that is on top of or underneath something else. Draw it on a sheet of paper, but don't show it to your partner. Your partner tries to guess what the object is by asking if it is on top of or underneath other things in the classroom. See how many questions your partner needs to ask before making the correct guess. Then switch roles.

> **MODELO** —**¿Está sobre el escritorio?**
>
> —**Sí.** *or* **No.**

CONEXIÓN CON LOS ESTUDIOS SOCIALES

Products Get together with a partner and read this article once.

Las frutas tropicales

En los países tropicales, hace calor y llueve mucho. Las temperaturas no cambian* mucho de una estación a otra. En esas regiones tropicales hay muchas frutas exóticas y deliciosas. El clima en muchos países de habla española es perfecto para las frutas tropicales. En esos países hay frutas como las papayas, los zapotes, las piñas, las granadillas, las guayabas y los mangos.

*change

Look at the globe. With a partner, make a list of the countries where you might find tropical fruit. Then describe the weather in these countries. Write in Spanish.

Entre amigos

Time for a game of **La cesta** ("The Basket"). It's a little like Musical Chairs.

The class sits on chairs in a circle, except for one student who stands in the middle. There must be an even number of students in the circle. Each student holds a picture of a fruit. You can cut these out of magazines or draw them. It is important that there be at least two pictures of every fruit.

The student in the middle asks a question with **poner** or **traer**—for example:

> **¿Qué traes en la cesta?**
> **¿Qué pone mamá en la cesta?**

Then he or she calls on someone to answer. The person who answers can name any fruit, as long as it's not the one in the picture he or she is holding.

> **Traigo una manzana en la cesta.**
> **Mamá pone unas uvas en la cesta.**

As soon as students hear their fruit mentioned, they must get up quickly and try to exchange seats with one another. But they need to hurry, because the student in the middle will be trying for one of their chairs, too! Whoever is left standing in the middle asks the next question.

En resumen

La sandía está **sobre** la mesa.
Juan pone el vaso **sobre** el televisor.

La sandía está **debajo de** la mesa.
Juan pone el vaso **debajo del** televisor.

¿Dónde se habla español?

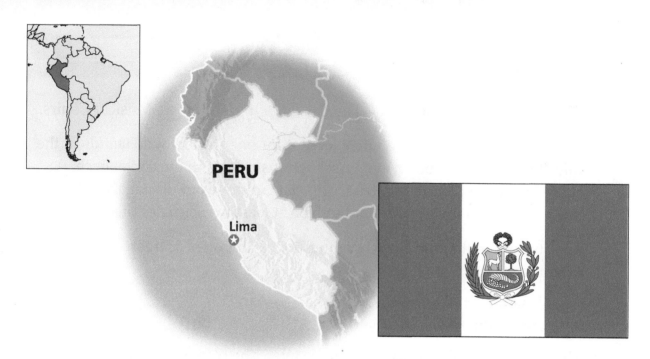

PERU

Lima ★

Perú

Peru is one of the most fascinating countries in South America. The Incan empire inhabited Peru for many centuries. Other pre-Columbian groups, like the Chimus, the Chavín, or the creators of the Nazca lines, lived there for hundreds of years. The incredible ruins of Machu Picchu are one of the archaeological wonders of the world. Peru's music, crafts, and foods reflect the Andean culture of the mountains, the culture of the Incas and other pre-Columbian groups, Spanish culture, and the Afro-Peruvian mixture of the coast.

When in Peru, you can sample foods like **anticuchos, papas rellenas, yucas, ceviche,** or **sopa a la criolla.** Inca Kola is a popular soft drink, and fruit juices are everywhere! The most popular flavors are pineapple, watermelon, orange, blackberry, and passion fruit.

Peru is also well known for its crafts: sweaters, ponchos, and belts made from alpaca and llama wool and beautifully designed and carved silver jewelry.

Datos

Capital: Lima

Ciudades importantes: Arequipa, El Callao, Chiclayo, Cuzco, Trujillo

Idiomas: Español, quechua, aymará

Moneda: El nuevo sol

Población: 28.4 millones

¡Léelo en español!

Machu Picchu y el Camino Inca

Machu Picchu está situado en las montañas Andes, cerca de Cuzco. Los arqueólogos piensan que era la casa de veraneo[1] de los reyes de los incas. Se puede caminar el Camino Inca[2] para ver las ruinas. El camino es de treinta y tres kilómetros. Para caminarlo, generalmente se toma[3] tres o cuatro días. Cuando llegas a Machu Picchu, vas a ver una ciudad emocionante.[4] Vas a pensar en los incas y en cómo vivieron.[5] Puedes sentarte en la Plaza Central. Puedes mirar el Templo del Sol, los baños ceremoniales, la Plaza Sagrada e Intihuatana, el santuario de Machu Picchu. Es un lugar misterioso y hermoso. Puedes comprender y apreciar la vida de los incas.

[1] summer   [2] The Inca Trail   [3] it takes
[4] exciting   [5] they lived

Reading Strategy

Using Context Clues Practice using clues from the subject matter, or context. When you read in a foreign language, there are going to be words that you do not know. Think about the subject matter and try to guess what they might mean by their use in the sentence. Guessing the meaning of words by how they are used is an important skill in learning a foreign language.

Recognizing Cognates What do you think these words mean: **arqueólogo, ceremoniales, santuario, apreciar?** Use these cognates to help you understand what is being said about Peru.

¡Comprendo!

Answer in English.

1. What are some of the cultures that have influenced modern Peruvian culture?

2. How would you need to prepare to hike the **Camino Inca?**

3. What are some of the important monuments that Machu Picchu is known for?

9

¿Qué quieres de desayuno?

Objetivos

- To talk about different kinds of breakfast foods and drinks

- To learn to talk about what you want

- To describe how much of something you want

- To talk about things you can and cannot do

- To discuss what belongs to you and to others

- To learn about some of the foods in Spanish-speaking countries

Huevos rancheros

An Argentinian reads the newspaper as he eats his breakfast.

Membrillo pastries and mate are a typical breakfast.

¿Sabías que...?

- Children in Spain don't usually have eggs for breakfast, but they do have them for lunch or dinner.

- Throughout Latin America, kids drink different things at breakfast: milk, juice, hot chocolate, and even coffee with milk (**el café con leche**).

- Mexico is famous for its big breakfasts, with items such as **huevos rancheros** (eggs with hot sauce), **tortillas,** and refried beans.

¿Cómo se dice?

¿Qué comes de desayuno?

—¿Qué comes de desayuno?

—Como huevos fritos.

los huevos revueltos

los huevos fritos

**los huevos pasados
por agua**

el cereal

la toronja

la avena

el pan tostado

la mermelada

la margarina

el jamón

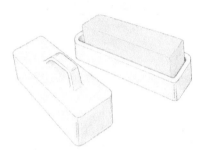

la mantequilla

el tocino

el queso

 CONEXIÓN CON LA CULTURA

Bread In Spanish-speaking countries, people go to the bakery daily to get freshly baked bread for their families. In most countries there is a great variety of breads and rolls. Some popular ones are "seashells" **(conchas),** "braids" **(trenzas),** and "half moons" **(medialunas).** Many people eat bread with every meal. Do you eat bread often? Who buys bread in *your* home?

¡Úsalo!

A Draw different breakfast foods that you know in Spanish on separate cards. Then get together with a partner, mix your cards, and put them facedown in a pile. Take turns asking each other what you'll have for breakfast. Pick a card and answer according to the drawing on it.

> **MODELO** —¿Qué comes de desayuno?
>
> —Como toronja.

B Get together with three or four classmates. One of you will be the "server." The server asks each "customer" what he or she will have and writes down the order. The customers pick something they'd like to eat. Take turns playing the server, and order different things each time!

> **MODELO** —¿Qué vas a comer?
>
> —Voy a comer pan tostado y mermelada.

¿Sabías que...?

In Cuba, there's a popular dish called **ropa vieja**. It uses leftover meat from other meals. It's usually served with rice and black beans, and it's delicious! Why do you think it's called **ropa vieja**?

CONEXIÓN CON LAS MATEMÁTICAS

Graphs Find out what your friends eat for breakfast, and how often.

Work with four or five classmates. Take turns asking one another if you eat the breakfast foods you've learned in Spanish. Use **siempre, a veces,** or **nunca** in your responses.

MODELO —¿Comes huevos fritos de desayuno?

—Sí, siempre como huevos fritos de desayuno.
or No, nunca como huevos fritos de desayuno.

Make a chart like this one to record your results. Assign 2 points for every **siempre** answer, 1 point for every **a veces** answer, and 0 points for every **nunca** answer. Then make a bar graph using these points to show the most popular and least popular foods.

	Siempre (2)	A veces (1)	Nunca (0)
huevos fritos	María		
cereal		Jorge, Luis	
pan tostado			
toronja			
avena			

En resumen

¿Qué **comes** de desayuno?
Como cereal.
    huevos fritos.
    huevos pasados por agua.
    huevos revueltos.
    jamón.
    pan tostado.
    queso.
    tocino.

Como avena.
    mantequilla.
    margarina.
    mermelada.
    toronja.

¿Cómo se dice?

¿Qué quieres beber?

—¿Qué quieres beber?
—Quiero leche, por favor.

 la leche

 el jugo

 el chocolate

 el café

 el té

 el agua

—¿Vas a tomar el desayuno?
—Sí, voy a tomar pan tostado
y café con leche.

tomar (el desayuno)

—¿Cuántos huevos hay?
—Hay pocos huevos. *or*
Hay muchos huevos.

—¿Hay huevos?
—No, no hay nada.

pocos huevos

muchos huevos

nada

CONEXIÓN CON LA SALUD

Balanced Breakfast Fresh milk, toast, and some fruit . . . there's no better way to start the day! A balanced breakfast should have a mix of carbohydrates, vitamins, and proteins. As you know, proteins are found in meat, eggs, and dairy products. Good sources of carbohydrates are grains. To get your share of vitamins, eat fruits or vegetables.

Two parts carbohydrates, one part proteins, and one part vitamins at breakfast gives you all the energy you will need to be alert and active for a busy day at school!

Sort these foods into the right categories. Some might go in two columns. Then, with a partner, see how many different balanced breakfasts you can make using these foods.

Proteínas	Carbohidratos	Vitaminas

fresas	queso	cereal
jugo de manzana	yogur	huevos fritos
jamón	leche	plátano
pera	pan tostado	huevos revueltos
avena	toronja	jugo de naranja

◎ ◎ ◎ ◎ Compara ◎ ◎ ◎ ◎

En inglés	En español
protein	la proteína
vitamin	la vitamina
carbohydrate	el carbohidrato
yogurt	el yogur

¡Úsalo!

A Get together with a partner. Look at the list below and think about what you'd like to drink in each situation. Take turns reading the sentences to each other about how you feel. Suggest a type of drink. Your partner answers according to what he or she prefers.

Partner A: Say how you feel, according to the list.

Partner B: Guess the drink your partner might have in that situation and ask about it.

> **MODELO** —Tengo sed.
>
> —¿Bebes agua?
>
> —Sí. *or* No, bebo té.

1. Tengo mucho frío.
2. Tengo mucho sueño.
3. Tengo calor.
4. Tengo la gripe.
5. Tengo mucha sed.
6. Tengo hambre.

B Make a weekly calendar like this one. Propose a different balanced breakfast for your family for each day. Complete the calendar with your and your family's favorite breakfast foods.

lunes	martes	miércoles	jueves	viernes	sábado	domingo
			huevos revueltos, pan tostado y jugo de manzana			

Now get together with a partner. Your partner asks what you and your family **(ustedes)** are going to have each day. Compare the breakfasts you chose.

> **MODELO** —¿Qué van a tomar de desayuno el jueves?
>
> —Vamos a tomar huevos revueltos, pan tostado y jugo de manzana.

¿Sabías que...?

The word **chocolate** came into the Spanish language (and then English) from the ancient language of the Aztecs, who lived in present-day Mexico. But you might not have recognized their version of the drink! The Aztecs used to drink it mixed with other seeds, and without sugar. They believed chocolate had medicinal powers and would keep them warm in winter.

Entre amigos

Get together with two or three classmates to create and design a breakfast menu for a restaurant. Use colors to make your menu come alive. Decorate it however you like. Be sure to give your restaurant a name.

Look at this restaurant's menu as an example:

Now take turns: one person plays the server, and the others play the customers. The server takes the customers' orders by asking what they want to eat and drink.

Restaurante Estrella

Desayuno
☆Huevos:
☆huevos fritos
☆huevos revueltos
☆huevos pasados por agua
☆cereal ☆pan tostado
☆chocolate ☆leche
☆jugo

En resumen

¿Vas a **tomar** el desayuno?
¿Qué **quieres** de desayuno?
beber?

Quiero mucha agua.
poca leche.
mucho café.
poco chocolate.
un jugo.
un té.

No hay nada.

¿Cómo se dice?

Talking about what you want and can do

These pictures and sentences show ways of saying that people want something.

Singular

Quiero un jugo, por favor.

Plural

Queremos dos jugos, por favor.

¿No **quieres** cereal?

¿**Quieren** ustedes chocolate?

Ella **quiere** avena.

Ellos **quieren** huevos revueltos.

To talk about wanting something, use the verb **querer.** Did you see that the **e** changed to **ie** in most of the forms of **querer?**

You can use **poco** and **mucho** to say how much you want of something.

Quiero **mucha** leche / **muchas** naranjas.   Quiero **poco** jugo / **pocos** plátanos.

You use these descriptive words *before* the word you describe. Use **-a** for feminine words and **-o** for masculine words. Add an **-s** to describe more than one thing.

Use **nada** to say that you want nothing. **Nada** never changes form. Notice that double negatives are used in Spanish: **No** quiero **nada.**

You can also use **querer** to talk about what you want to do:

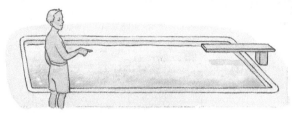

Quiero nadar ahora.

Queremos tomar chocolate.

Another important verb in Spanish is **poder,** which means "to be able to." Here's how you use it:

Singular

Puedo cantar.

Plural

Podemos bailar.

¡Puedes pintar muy bien!

¿Ustedes **pueden** cocinar?

Puede caminar.

Pueden correr.

To say that someone can or can't do something, use a form of **poder** + another verb.

Did you see that the **o** changed to **ue** in most of the forms of **poder?** What other verbs do you know that do that?

CONEXIÓN CON LOS ESTUDIOS SOCIALES

Trade More than half of the coffee imported into the United States in the year 2000 came from Latin America. Put these countries in order, from the largest exporter to the smallest.

México: 2,389,248 bags
Costa Rica: 915,797 bags
Honduras: 507,852 bags
Guatemala: 2,187,427 bags

El Salvador: 613,064 bags
Colombia: 3,307,959 bags
Perú: 661,231 bags

(In 60 kilogram bags) Source: USDA

Compara	
En inglés	**En español**
to import	importar

¡Úsalo!

A Cut out ten pictures of breakfast foods from magazines. Now get together with a partner and place all the pictures on the table. Take turns asking each other what you want for breakfast. Pick three of the foods. Your partner puts the items on a paper plate and "serves" them to you.

> **MODELO** —¿Qué quieres de desayuno?
>
> —Quiero cereal con leche y jugo de manzana.

B Imagine that it's Saturday. Write down what you want for breakfast. Add something you could do with a friend afterward.

Get in a circle with four or five classmates. Take turns asking the person to your right what he or she wants for breakfast. Then ask what you can do together afterward. The person answers according to what he or she wrote. Use forms of **querer** and **poder** in your answers.

C Tomorrow is a busy day! Make a schedule like this one and write in five or six things you will do tomorrow. Include activities in the morning, afternoon, and evening. Now get together with a partner and see if your partner can join you for any of these activities, according to his or her schedule.

lunes		lunes
A.M. **8:00**		1:30
8:15		1:45
8:30		**2:00**
8:45		2:15
9:00		2:30
9:15		2:45
9:30		**3:00**
9:45		3:15
10:00		3:30
10:15		3:45
10:30		**4:00**
10:45		4:15
11:00		4:30
11:15		4:45
11:30		**5:00**
11:45		5:15
P.M.		5:30
12:00		5:45
12:15		**6:00**
12:30		6:15
12:45		6:30
1:00		6:45
1:15		**7:00**

MODELO —¿Puedes nadar a las tres de la tarde?

—Ummm... No, no puedo. Tengo que estudiar a las tres. *or* Sí, podemos nadar a las tres.

Entre amigos

Your teacher will distribute breakfast cards to everyone. There will be several cards for each type of food, and several that say **el camarero / la camarera** ("the server").

Go around the classroom asking people what they want for breakfast. They must answer according to what's on their card. Find all the people who have the same card as you and get together in a group.

In the meantime, the servers prepare a menu of available breakfast items.

Then the servers go to each group and ask them what they want for breakfast. Someone from each group answers for all of them **(nosotros)**. The server answers according to the menu.

—¿Qué quieren de desayuno?
—Queremos huevos fritos.
—No hay huevos fritos. *or* Hay huevos fritos.

CONEXIÓN CON LAS MATEMÁTICAS

Money You need to go to the store to buy breakfast for your mom, your dad, your brothers and sister, and yourself. This is a list of what your family wants. Think of what you want for yourself and write it down.

Mamá	Pan tostado, 2 huevo fritos, un café con leche
Papá	3 huevos revueltos, jugo de naranja, un café
Laura	1 bol de cereal, jugo de naranja
Iván	Pan tostado con mantequilla, 1 huevo pasado por agua
José	2 huevos pasados por agua
Yo	

First, decide what you have to buy and look at the prices. Then figure out how much money you need to take to the store. (**Una libra** means "a pound" and **un frasco** means "a jar.") What bills will you bring? How much change will you have left over?

Pan (1 libra)	$0.85	Cereal (1 caja)	$5.00
Huevos (1 docena)	$1.50	Jugo de naranja (1 litro)	$2.00
Leche (1 litro)	$1.80	Mermelada (1 frasco)	$2.80
Mantequilla (1 libra)	$2.45	Café (1 libra)	$5.00

Compara

En inglés	En español
dozen	la docena
package	el paquete
liter	el litro

En resumen

	e → ie	o → ue
	querer	**poder**
(Yo)	qu**ie**ro	p**ue**do + caminar
(Tú)	qu**ie**res	p**ue**des
(Él, Ella, Ud.)	qu**ie**re	p**ue**de
(Nosotros, Nosotras)	quer**emos**	pod**emos**
(Ellos, Ellas, Uds.)	qu**ie**ren	p**ue**den

¿Cómo se dice?

Talking about possessions

You already know how to talk about things that belong to you.

| **mi** radio | **mis** radios | **mi** escoba | **mis** escobas |

You also know how to talk to a friend about his or her possessions **(tu radio, tus escobas)** and how to talk about things that belong to somebody else **(su radio, sus escobas).**

Now look at how you talk about things that belong to both you and another person ("our").

| **nuestro** radio | **nuestros** radios | **nuestra** escoba | **nuestras** escobas |

Use **nuestro** and **nuestros** with masculine words, and use **nuestra** and **nuestras** with feminine words.

Which word do you use with the word **camas—nuestros** or **nuestras?** How about with the word **televisores?** It's easy, once you know if the word is masculine or feminine, singular or plural.

Now look at these pictures and sentences. They show you how to talk about things that belong to several other people—"their."

Su casa es grande.

Sus cuadros son bonitos.

Su is used with masculine and feminine words. Add an **-s** if you're saying people own more than one of something.

¿Sabías que...?

You've probably seen Mexican **tortillas**—flat pieces of bread made out of flour or corn. But for Spanish speakers, it means other things as well! **Tortilla** means "omelette" in many places. In Spain, **la tortilla española** is a popular dish made with eggs, onion, and potatoes fried in olive oil. For Chileans, it means unleavened bread.

¡Úsalo!

A Get together with two classmates. Each of you secretly puts five belongings into the same bag. Then you sit in a circle. The first person pulls out an item. If it belongs to the person, he or she says so. If not, the first person asks if it belongs to the second person, and if not, to the third person. Place each item in front of its owner as you pull it out.

> **MODELO** —Es mi libro. *or* ¿Es tu libro?
>
> —Sí, es mi libro. *or* No, no es mi libro.

B Your family just moved, but the moving truck brought the wrong boxes. You're talking to the moving company and describing your family's belongings. Use the list of things below—or make up your own—and **nuestro, nuestros, nuestra,** or **nuestras** to describe your belongings to a partner. Your partner draws the different items you mention. Then, switch roles.

> **MODELO** horno negro
>
> **Nuestro horno es negro.**

1. sofá gris
2. cortinas blancas
3. televisor pequeño
4. mesas grandes
5. estufa amarilla
6. muebles marrones

CONEXIÓN CON LA CULTURA

Family Extended families in the Spanish-speaking world tend to be very close. Cousins see each other often, may go to school together, and borrow things from each other. It's common for siblings and cousins to get together to play sports, eat, and have fun! How about you? Do you see your cousins often? Do you go out more with your friends or with your family?

C Ask your partner these questions. Your partner will answer. Use your partner's answers to make a shopping list of the things that he or she might want to buy.

1. ¿Son nuevos o viejos tus muebles?

2. ¿Es grande tu televisor?

3. ¿Son nuevas o viejas tus camas?

4. ¿Es bonita tu alfombra?

5. ¿Cómo es tu refrigerador?

6. ¿De qué color es tu horno?

7. ¿Son nuevas tus lámparas?

8. ¿Cómo son tus espejos?

9. ¿Cómo son tus cortinas?

10. ¿Cómo son tus radios?

D You're picking up some things for the López family. Make ten cards with drawings of different household items. Draw several of the same items on some cards. Write **los López** on the back of *half* of the cards.

Get together with a partner, mix up the cards, and put them facedown in a pile. Your partner picks one and asks you if the item(s) belongs to the López family. Answer according to what is written on the back.

Partner A: Ask if the items you picked belong to the López family.

Partner B: Answer according to what is on the back of the card.

MODELO —¿Son sus cortinas?

—Sí, son sus cortinas. *or* No, no son sus cortinas.

Entre amigos

Get together in a circle with five or six classmates.

One person starts by telling the group about breakfast in his or her house:

—En nuestra casa tomamos de desayuno huevos revueltos y jugo de naranja.

Be sure to mention one item you eat and one you drink. Now the next person to the left does the same thing. Be careful, though, not to mention the same combination of drink and food items.

Keep going around the circle, saying what you eat and drink for breakfast in your house. Keep track of the answers people give. The game ends when someone mentions a food or drink combination that has been mentioned before, but you can start over if there is time.

En resumen

mi radio	**mis** radios
mi escoba	**mis** escobas
tu radio	**tus** radios
tu escoba	**tus** escobas
nuestro radio	**nuestros** radios
nuestra escoba	**nuestras** escobas
su radio	**sus** radios
su escoba	**sus** escobas

¿Dónde se habla español?

La Paz

BOLIVIA

Bolivia
(República de Bolivia)

Bolivia is sometimes called the Tibet of the Americas. It is set high in the Andes mountains and is full of natural beauty. Many indigenous people still live there. Like Peru, it was part of the great Incan empire.

Bolivia has many parks and preserves where you can see all types of animals and plants. Bolivia is also rich in natural resources like tin, copper, silver and gold. Two Andean mountain ranges run through the country. In the middle of them is an immense, flat area called the **Altiplano.** Most Bolivians live in the **Altiplano** and their typical music, dance, and dress come from that area.

Bolivia's national dance is called the **cueca.** It is danced by couples who wave handkerchiefs. Andean music as played by the native Andeans is often instrumental and involves instruments like reed flutes, pan flutes, and **sikus.** Bolivian weavings are colorful and made by hand in many patterns. The colorful woven hat of the Andean natives is typical of the Bolivian **Altiplano.**

Datos

Capital: La Paz

Ciudades importantes: Sucre, Cochabamba, Oruro, Santa Cruz de la Sierra, Potosí

Idiomas: Español, quechua, aymará, tupí-guaraní

Moneda: El boliviano

Población: 8.6 millones

¡Léelo en español!

El lago Titicaca El lago Titicaca está en la frontera[1] de Perú y Bolivia. Si miras el mapa de América del Sur, puedes ver el lago Titicaca fácilmente[2] porque es muy grande. Es el lago navegable más alto del mundo y está en el Altiplano de Bolivia. Es de muchos colores bonitos y claros de azul y verde.

Según[3] algunas leyendas de los indígenas, el Sol nació[4] en este lago. Hay truchas[5], un tipo de pescado, muy grandes en el lago. La gente come la trucha y los restaurantes sirven la trucha.

La isla más grande del lago es la Isla del Sol. Los incas piensan que su dios blanco con barba apareció[6] aquí. Es un lugar sagrado[7] para los indígenas.

[1] border   [2] easily   [3] according to   [4] was born
[5] trout   [6] appeared   [7] sacred

¿Dónde se habla español?

Reading Strategy

Skimming Before reading a selection, skim the passage, that is, read it quickly to find out the general ideas of the passage. If possible, discuss those ideas. Then read the passage for details.

Using Cognates What do you think these words mean: **mapa, leyendas, isla?** Use these cognates to help you understand what is being said about Bolivia.

¡Comprendo!

Answer in English.

1. When you skim the passage, list the two general topics being discussed. (Hint: Two places are being described.)

2. What legends surround Lake Titicaca and its islands? Why do you think these places are considered sacred?

3. Why is Bolivia sometimes called the Tibet of the Americas?

4. What is the **Altiplano?**

¡Queremos almorzar!

Objetivos

- To talk about foods you eat for lunch and dinner
- To discuss when you eat meals
- To talk about special likes and dislikes
- To learn about some of the foods in Spanish-speaking countries

Fresh and dried chile peppers and chile powder

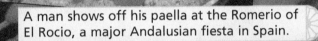
A man shows off his paella at the Romerio of El Rocio, a major Andalusian fiesta in Spain.

¿Sabías que...?

- There is an enormous variety of dishes in Spanish-speaking countries. They range from very mild, delicate recipes to very hot and spicy foods.

- Beans, corn, and rice are food items that are widely used in almost every Spanish-speaking country.

- **Chiles** (hot peppers), considered a fruit, are an ingredient used in many traditional Mexican dishes. There are more than 1,000 varieties of **chiles** that vary in size, color, and flavor.

A person makes stone-ground Mexican tortillas.

¿Cómo se dice?

¿Qué quieres de almuerzo?

—¿Qué quieres de almuerzo?
—Quiero una ensalada.

el almuerzo

la ensalada

el tomate

la lechuga

el pollo

la papa

la hamburguesa

el sándwich

el pan

la crema de cacahuate

las verduras

la mayonesa

la mostaza

la salsa de tomate

¿Sabías que...?

In many Spanish-speaking countries, lunch is eaten later than in the United States, sometimes as late as 3:00 in the afternoon. It can be a large meal with soup, meat or fish, vegetables, rice, beans, salad, and then dessert and coffee.

Digestive System You may forget about lunch once you're finished eating, but the food you eat stays in your body for a while! Food gives you nutrients to keep you healthy, and energy so you can do your daily activities. But first it has to go through the process of digestion.

Here are the parts of the body that food goes through before being absorbed into your bloodstream for delivery to your cells.

Get together with a partner and put the parts of the body that aid in digestion in order, from first to last. Then decide where each part goes in the diagram.

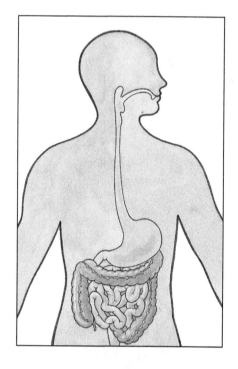

estómago, esófago, boca, intestino grueso*, intestino delgado*

*grueso = large; delgado = small

◎ ◎ ◎ **Compara** ◎ ◎ ◎	
En inglés	**En español**
stomach	el estómago
esophagus	el esófago
intestine	el intestino

¿Sabías que...?

Dinner times vary from country to country throughout the Spanish-speaking world. In Mexico, dinner is served between 7:00 and 8:00 p. m. Children in Spain don't eat dinner until 9:00 or 10:00 p. m.! Because they have a big lunch, at night they have a light meal, and soon afterward they're off to bed.

¡Úsalo!

Do you have a good memory? It's always a good idea to remember what people like! Get together with four or five classmates. Each person asks the person to the right what he or she likes to eat for lunch on weekends.

MODELO —¿Qué te gusta comer de almuerzo los fines de semana?

—Me gusta comer pollo y papas.

Now everyone in the group says what the person to his or her right likes.

MODELO —A Arturo le gusta comer pollo y papas los fines de semana.

Entre amigos

Enter a cook-off! Get together with three or four classmates. Choose the best dish you can think of, based on all the foods you know.

Together, make a poster of your meal. Make it as attractive as possible, so that you can convince people to choose it. You can draw a picture of your meal or cut out photos from magazines.

Now put your poster on the board with a name and a number. Once everyone's posters are in place, a volunteer asks each student what he or she would like to eat for lunch.

¿Qué quieres de almuerzo?

The volunteer notes the vote on the board.

The catch is, you can't vote for your own group's dish!

The dish with the most votes wins the cook-off. You can also take your posters to the school cafeteria and have other students vote for their favorite dish as well.

CONEXIÓN CON LA SALUD

Food Hygiene You wash your hands before eating to get rid of germs. But don't forget to wash your food! Crops are sprayed with pesticides so that bugs won't ruin them. And many people handle food, so if you eat the peels or skins, you'd better wash them before eating!

Make a chart like the one below and sort these foods into two groups: those that need to be washed **(se lavan)** and those that don't. Remember that you don't need to wash it if you have to remove the peel or skin! Compare your chart to a partner's.

se lavan	no se lavan

los plátanos   las cerezas   las peras

las sandías   las piñas   los tomates

el pollo   los duraznos   las fresas

la avena   las toronjas   las manzanas

la lechuga   las papas   el pan

las uvas   las naranjas

En resumen

el almuerzo	la crema de cacahuate
el pan	la ensalada
el pollo	la hamburguesa
el sándwich	la lechuga
el tomate	la mayonesa
	la mostaza
	la papa
	la salsa de tomate
	las verduras

¿Cómo se dice?

¿Qué hay de cena?

—¿Qué hay de cena?
—Hay arroz y pescado.

la cena

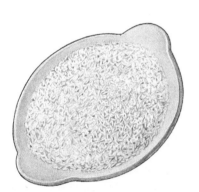

el arroz

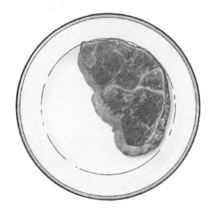

la carne

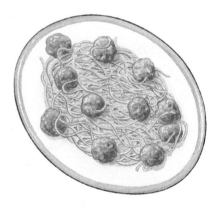

los espaguetis
con albóndigas

el pavo

el pescado

la sopa

—¿Te gustan los guisantes?

—Sí, pero me gusta más el maíz.

los guisantes

el maíz

las zanahorias

los frijoles

el helado

el pastel

 ## CONEXIÓN CON LOS ESTUDIOS SOCIALES

Argentinian Beef Argentinian children and their families enjoy getting together and eating **asado,** a kind of barbecue. Argentinian beef is among the best in the world. Cows have plenty of space to graze in the grassy plains known as **la pampa.** Argentina has a long cattle-raising tradition, and beef has always been one of the country's main exports. What are the most important cattle-raising states in the United States?

¡Úsalo!

A Draw five foods you know on different cards. Then put your cards in a box along with those of the rest of the class. Everyone picks five cards. Take turns going around the classroom to find other students with matching cards.

> **MODELO** —Michael, ¿quieres arroz de cena?
>
> —Sí, gracias. *or* No, gracias.

When you find a matching card, give your card to that person. The one who gets rid of his or her cards first wins!

B Work with a partner and make a dinner menu for each night of the week. Pick a main course, at least one side dish, and a dessert. Look at these sample menus for **lunes** and **martes.**

After you finish, share your meal plans with other pairs.

> **MODELO** —¿Qué hay de cena el lunes?
>
> —Hay carne, papas, guisantes y sandía.

lunes:

carne
papas
guisantes
sandía

martes:

pollo
sopa
arroz
piña
helado
pastel

¿Sabías que...?

People all over the Spanish-speaking world love rice! Typical rice dishes include Spanish **paella** and **arroz negro** (rice with squid ink) and Puerto Rican and Cuban **arroz con pollo** and **asopao** (a hearty stew). Rice can even be made into a popular dessert called **arroz con leche!**

C Get together with a partner. Use these pictures to ask your partner if he or she likes these foods, then ask which ones he or she likes more. Ask questions until you can list these foods in order from most favorite to least favorite. Then switch roles.

> **MODELO** —¿Te gustan los guisantes?
>
> —Sí.
>
> —¿Cuál te gusta más, los guisantes o el pescado?
>
> —Me gustan más los guisantes. *or* Me gusta más el pescado.

1.

2.
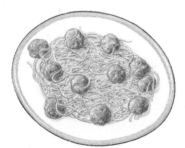

3.

4.

5.

6.

D Design your ideal birthday meal. Get together with three classmates. Be creative! Choose a main dish, two side dishes, something to drink, and a dessert (**el postre**). Present your menu to the class.

> **MODELO** Vamos a tomar helado con crema de cacahuate y mermelada. Vamos a beber mucho jugo de uva. De postre, vamos a comer hamburguesas con queso, y también ¡un pastel de pescado!

CONEXIÓN CON LA SALUD

Nutrition Get together with a partner and read the article below. Help each other figure out the unfamiliar words.

La buena comida para la buena salud

Hay cinco grupos básicos de comida: pan, cereal, arroz y pasta; frutas; verduras; carne, pescado, frijoles, huevos y nueces; leche, yogur y queso. Cada día tienes que comer algo de cada grupo. Estas comidas tienen las vitaminas, los minerales y las proteínas para mantener la buena salud.

Pan, cereal, arroz, pasta	Frutas	Verduras	Carne, pescado, frijoles, huevos, nueces	Leche, yogur, queso
pan	plátanos	zanahorias	jamón	leche
arroz	mangos	guisantes	frijoles	queso
tortilla	chiles		huevos	yogur
cereal			pollo	helado
avena			carne	crema

With your partner, put together five different meals that include at least one food from each group. You may use the foods from the chart, or any others you know. Make sure you put them in the right group! Get together with another pair and ask them whether they like your meals. Find out which one they like more.

En resumen

el arroz
el helado
el maíz
el pastel
el pavo
el pescado
los espaguetis con albóndigas
los frijoles
los guisantes

la carne
la cena
la sopa
las zanahorias

¿Cómo se dice?

Talking about having lunch

The verb that means "to have lunch" is **almorzar.** Read the sentences to see how to use it. See if you can tell why **almorzar** is different from regular **-ar** verbs.

| **Singular** | **Plural** |

Yo **almuerzo** al mediodía.

Nosotros **almorzamos** a las dos.

¿Almuerzas a las once?

¿Almuerzan ustedes a la una?

Ella **almuerza** a la una y media.

Diego y Carolina **almuerzan**
al mediodía.

Did you notice that the letter **o** changes to **ue** in most of the forms of **almorzar?** The only form that doesn't change in this way is the **nosotros** form **(almorzamos).**

The verb **probar**, which means "to taste" or "to try," is another verb that is like **almorzar:**

Pruebo la sopa.

Probamos los espaguetis.

How would you ask a friend if he's tasting something? How would you say that someone else is tasting something?

CONEXIÓN CON LA CULTURA

Mexican Food You may have eaten at a Mexican restaurant in the United States. But even though the meal was tasty, did you know that some of the food you've tried is not authentic Mexican food? Like other types of cooking, Mexican food has been adapted in the United States. Most of the Mexican food here is based on traditional Mexican cooking, but with ingredients available in the United States, and adapted to U.S. tastes.

¡Úsalo!

A Make a chart like this one and fill it out with information about lunchtimes for yourself and your relatives. If you don't know something, you can make it up! Then get together with a partner. Ask each other questions to compare family lunchtimes.

> **MODELO** —¿A qué hora almuerza tu abuela?
>
> —Mi abuela almuerza a las doce del mediodía.
>
> —Mi abuela almuerza a las dos.

EL ALMUERZO	Mi abuela	Mis padres	Yo (los sábados)
¿A qué hora...?			
¿Qué...?			
¿Dónde...?			

B You're in the school cafeteria and see the new Friday menu. Try it out! Sit in a circle with five or six classmates. Each of you writes two foods you want to try. Now go around the circle and say what you're trying. Keep track on a list like the one on the right.

> **MODELO** —Pruebo la ensalada y el maíz.

Now take turns saying things that *two* people are trying today.

> **MODELO** —Silvia y Juan prueban las hamburguesas. *or* Ramón y yo probamos las peras.

M E N Ú	
ensalada	
pescado	
hamburguesas	Silvia, Juan
guisantes	
zanahorias	
maíz	
papas	
peras	Ramón, yo

CONEXIÓN CON LA SALUD

Cooking Safety Uncooked meat can harbor harmful bacteria. It's important to cook it at the right temperature. This way, possible bacteria are killed. Each type of meat has a different safe cooking temperature.

	Temperatura
carne roja	160°F
pollo	190°F
jamón	160°F

Look at these pictures. Say the temperature and decide with a partner whether the food is safe to try.

1.

2.

3.
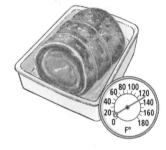

MODELO —La temperatura es de ciento diez grados Fahrenheit.

—¿Probamos?

—No.

En resumen

	o → ue
	almorz**ar**
(Yo)	alm**ue**rzo
(Tú)	alm**ue**rz**as**
(Él, Ella, Ud.)	alm**ue**rza
(Nosotros, Nosotras)	almorz**amos**
(Ellos, Ellas, Uds.)	alm**ue**rz**an**

¿Cómo se dice?

Who likes what?

You've already learned how to use the verb **gustar** to talk about what you like, to ask a friend what he or she likes, and to say what someone else likes.

—¿**Te gusta** el maíz?
—Sí, **me gusta** el maíz.

—¿**Te gustan** las verduras?
—No, no **me gustan** las verduras.

—¿A Marina **le gusta** el pescado?
—Sí, **le gusta** el pescado.

Now look at these sentences to see how to say that you and someone else like something.

Nos gusta la ensalada.

Nos gustan las verduras.

And here's how to say that several other people like something, or more than one thing.

Les gusta el queso.

Les gustan las papas fritas.

If you want to ask who likes something, you ask **¿A quién le gusta... ?**

¿A quién le gusta el helado?

A nosotros nos gusta el helado.

A ellas les gusta el helado.

To be very clear about who likes something, Spanish speakers use **a** + *a person's name* or a word that stands for a person's name, such as **él, ella, nosotros, nosotras,** or **ustedes.** When talking about yourself or talking to a friend, use **a mí** or **a ti:**

A mí me gusta el helado.
¿A ti te gusta el helado?

CONEXIÓN CON LA CULTURA

Celebrations People around the world celebrate in different ways—but celebrations always involve food! For special occasions, Puerto Ricans might have a whole pig roast. Argentinians may roast a whole cow! Spaniards might celebrate with a **paella.** How does *your* family celebrate special occasions?

¡Úsalo!

A Now it's your turn to be a chef! Get together with three classmates. Take turns asking your classmates what they like and don't like. Ask about as many foods as you can, so that you'll have more to work with!

> **MODELO** —¿Te gustan los guisantes?
>
> —Sí, me gustan. *or* No, no me gustan.

Now "make" your dish by combining everyone's favorite foods and drawing the dish on a paper plate. Color it, give it a name, and show it to your group. Summarize the things that people in the group like as you present it.

> **MODELO** **Son papas fritas con salsa de tomate.**
> **A Ana y a Pablo les gustan las papas.**
> **A Raquel le gusta la salsa de tomate.**

B You're going to interview several classmates and your teacher to complete the sentences below. Before interviewing them, get together with a partner to think of questions that will help you find these answers.

1. A mí me gustan _____.

2. A mi amigo(a) no le gusta _____.

3. A mí y a mi amigo nos gusta _____ y no nos gustan _____.

4. A _____ y a _____ les gustan _____ y no les gusta _____.

5. A mi maestro(a) le gusta _____ y no le gusta _____.

CONEXIÓN CON LA SALUD

Food Guide Pyramid The food guide pyramid is an easy way to show the mix of foods that's most healthful for you.

Help create a food guide pyramid. Your teacher will draw a large pyramid on a bulletin board in the room.

Now look for pictures of food in magazines, supermarket ads, and newspapers. Cut out ten different types of food. Make a chart like this one and write the names of your foods in the right categories.

Pan, cereal, arroz y pasta	Frutas	Verduras	Carne, pescado, frijoles, huevos y nueces	Leche, yogur y queso

Are you missing foods for any category? Start searching!

Now take turns going to the bulletin board and placing your food pictures in the correct part of the pyramid. Name the ones you know and tell which ones you like and dislike.

En resumen

Me gusta **el** helado.	Me gusta**n** **las** cereza**s**.
Te gusta	Te gusta**n**
Le gusta	Le gusta**n**
Nos gusta	Nos gusta**n**
Les gusta	Les gusta**n**

¿Dónde se habla español?

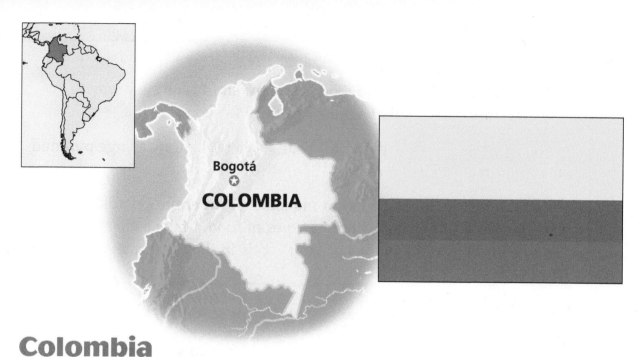

Bogotá
COLOMBIA

Colombia
(República de Colombia)

Colombia is the land of coffee, emeralds and gold. In Bogotá there is a museum **(el Museo del Oro)** full of over 33,000 gold pieces from the major pre-Hispanic cultures of Colombia. You will also find an underground cathedral carved out of solid salt inside a mountain.

Many people think the best coffee comes from Colombia. In addition to coffee, there are many typical dishes to try on a visit to Colombia. Soups, fruit of all types, and barbecued chicken are readily available.

Gabriel García Márquez is a famous author from Colombia. His novels have been translated and enjoyed throughout the world. The most famous of these is *One Hundred Years of Solitude,* or **Cien años de soledad.**

◎◎◎◎ Datos ◎◎◎◎

Capital: Bogotá

Ciudades importantes: Barranquilla, Cali, Cartagena, Medellín

Idiomas: Español, idiomas indígenas

Moneda: El peso colombiano

Población: 41.7 millones

¡Léelo en español!

Los piratas del Caribe Cartagena es una ciudad en el norte de Colombia. Cartagena se fundó[1] en 1533 como una puerta del Caribe. Los españoles trajeron[2] oro y tesoros a esta ciudad para poner en los barcos. Los barcos llevaban[3] el oro y los tesoros a España. Muchos piratas sabían[4] eso y atacaban[5] la ciudad y los barcos. Robaban[6] el oro y los tesoros. El más famoso de los piratas fue Sir Francis Drake.

El cantante Juanes Juanes es un cantante moderno y famoso. Es de Medellín, Colombia, pero ahora vive en Los Ángeles. Su nombre viene de dos nombres, Juan y Esteban. Canta desde los siete años. Su padre y sus cinco hermanos son sus profesores de música. Canta canciones románticas, de rock y de influencias folklóricas.

En el año 2003 gana cinco Grammys latinos. Juanes es moreno, guapo y simpático. Cuando vino[7] a la ciudad de Los Ángeles en los Estados Unidos, no tenía[8] mucho dinero, sólo su música. Con su música gana dinero y fama. Sus canciones son muy populares.

---

[1] was founded [2] brought [3] carried [4] knew
[5] attacked [6] They robbed [7] he came
[8] he didn't have

¡Comprendo!

Answer in English.
Summarize each of the passages on the left, first to a partner and then write your summary on paper. Be sure to address the following questions:

1. Where is Cartagena and what is its historical importance?

2. Who is Juanes?

3. How has his life changed since he was a child?

INSTITUCION
EDUCATIVA LUIS FELIPE CA
FE Y ALEGR

FE Y ALEGRIA

Todos los días. . .

Objetivos

- To talk about your daily routines

- To talk about other activities you do

- To discuss things you do for yourself and things others do for themselves

Luis Felipe Cabrera school in Barú, Colombia

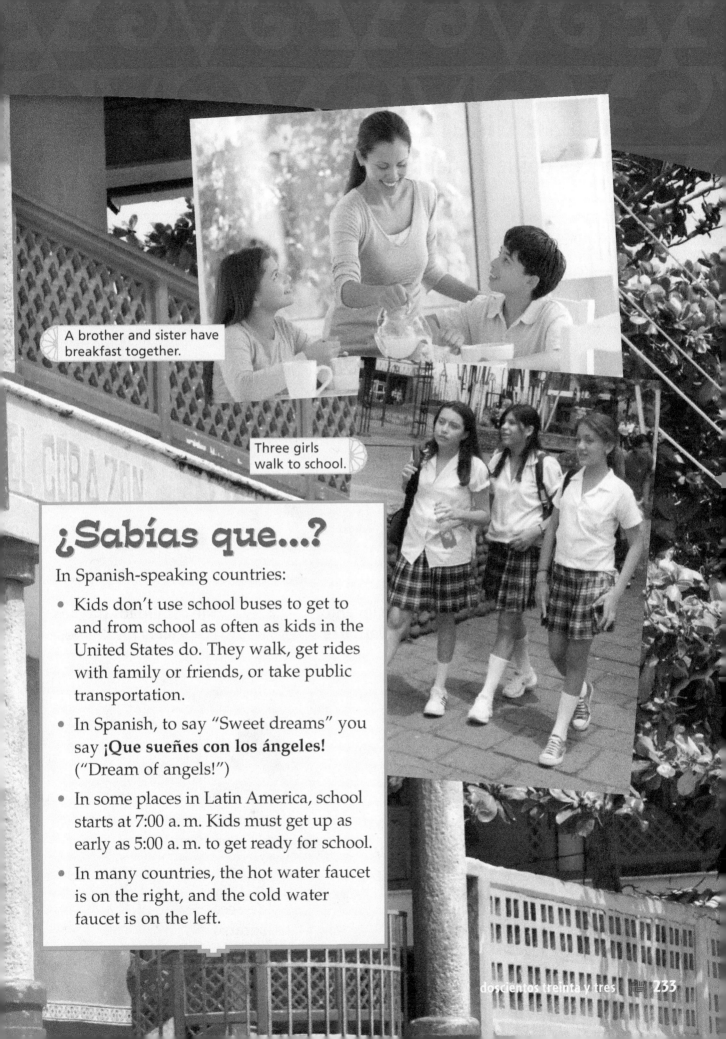

A brother and sister have breakfast together.

Three girls walk to school.

¿Sabías que...?

In Spanish-speaking countries:

- Kids don't use school buses to get to and from school as often as kids in the United States do. They walk, get rides with family or friends, or take public transportation.

- In Spanish, to say "Sweet dreams" you say ¡Que sueñes con los ángeles! ("Dream of angels!")

- In some places in Latin America, school starts at 7:00 a. m. Kids must get up as early as 5:00 a. m. to get ready for school.

- In many countries, the hot water faucet is on the right, and the cold water faucet is on the left.

¿Cómo se dice?

¿Qué haces por la mañana?

—¿Qué haces por la mañana?

—Primero me despierto. Luego me levanto y me cepillo los dientes...

Me despierto.
despertarse

Me levanto.
levantarse

Me cepillo los dientes.
cepillarse los dientes

Me lavo.
lavarse

Me seco.
secarse

Me pongo la ropa.
ponerse la ropa

Me peino.
peinarse

—Y por último, ¿qué haces?
—Por último, me voy a la escuela.

Me voy a la escuela.
irse a la escuela

¿Sabías que...?

Spanish speakers use many expressions that contain the word **espejo.** For example, **Mírate en ese espejo** (literally "Look at yourself in that mirror") means "Let what happened be an example to you." When something is spotless, you can say **Está limpio como un espejo.** If you look at someone **(mirarse en una persona) como en un espejo,** this means that you look up to the person.

¡Úsalo!

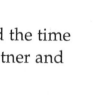

5:00 a.m.	7:00 a.m. Tomo el desayuno
5:30 a.m.	7:30 a.m.
6:00 a.m.	8:00 a.m.
6:30 a.m.	8:30 a.m.

A Write a list of things you do each morning and the time you do each one. Then get together with a partner and compare your schedules.

> **MODELO** —Me despierto a las seis de la mañana.
>
> —Yo también. *or* Yo me despierto a las seis y media.

B On different cards, draw all the activities you do each morning. Then mix the cards together and hand them to a partner. Your partner asks you about your activities and puts the cards in order. Then switch roles.

> **MODELO** —¿Qué haces primero?
>
> —Primero, me levanto y me lavo la cara.
>
> —¿Y luego?
>
> —Luego, me cepillo los dientes.

CONEXIÓN CON LA SALUD

Dental Hygiene Conduct a survey to find out if your classmates are taking good care of their teeth. Ask everyone in your class these questions.

	siempre	a veces	nunca
¿Te cepillas los dientes por la mañana?		✔ ✔	
¿Te cepillas los dientes por la noche?			

Get together with a partner to compare the results. Give 2 points for each **siempre** answer, 1 point for each **a veces** answer, and 0 points for each **nunca** answer. Add the points and divide by the number of students in the class to find the average. Determine whether most of your classmates are brushing regularly or if they need to improve their dental hygiene.

CONEXIÓN CON LOS ESTUDIOS SOCIALES

Timeline Create a vertical timeline of a typical morning in your life. Divide your line into quarters of an hour. Write the things you need to do at each time, from the moment you wake up to the time you leave for school.

Then get together with a partner and exchange timelines. Look at your partner's timeline and ask him or her about the different entries to make sure they are correct.

MODELO —¿Tomas el desayuno a las seis y media?

 # Entre amigos

Your teacher will lead you in a version of **Simón dice.** Listen carefully, and do the actions that Simón does himself. Be sure to do only the actions that start with **Simón dice** and the **yo** form of the verb!

Simón dice... me pongo la ropa.

Now take turns leading the game.

En resumen

Me cepillo los dientes.	**cepillarse**
Me despierto.	**despertarse**
Me voy a la escuela.	**irse**
Me lavo.	**lavarse**
Me levanto.	**levantarse**
Me peino.	**peinarse**
Me pongo la ropa.	**ponerse**
Me seco.	**secarse**

¿Cómo se dice?

¿Qué haces por la noche?

—¿Qué haces por la noche?

—Primero vuelvo a la casa.

Vuelvo a la casa.
volver

Me quito la ropa.
quitarse

Me ducho.
ducharse

Me acuesto.
acostarse

Me baño.
bañarse

CONEXIÓN CON EL ARTE

Painting A favorite theme in art is portraying people doing day-to-day things, such as brushing their hair, looking in the mirror, or giving a child a bath. Look at these paintings and describe what you see to a partner. Then make your own work of art of a person doing an everyday activity. Try to imitate one of the styles you see here.

¡Úsalo!

A Think of possible things you might do at these times. Share your activities with a partner.

> MODELO —A las 12:30 de la tarde, almuerzo.

1. A las 3:30 de la tarde, _____.

2. A las 6:00 de la tarde, _____.

3. A las 8:30 de la noche, _____.

4. A las 9:00 de la noche, _____.

5. A las 9:30 de la noche, _____.

¿Sabías que...?

In some countries, like Spain and Argentina, bedtimes tend to be late. Since dinner often isn't until 8:00 p. m. or 9:00 p. m., kids usually don't go to bed before 10:30 p. m., even on school nights.

B Make a chart like this one and fill it in. Write the time when you do each activity. Then get together with two classmates and ask them when they do these activities.

> **MODELO** —¿Cuándo vuelves a casa?
>
> —Vuelvo a casa a las seis de la tarde.

	Yo	Sandra	Manuel	Francisco
volver a casa				
quitarse la ropa				
cenar				
hablar por teléfono				
bañarse / ducharse				
cepillarse los dientes				
acostarse				

Then compare your schedules and write sentences saying what one or two students do and what you all do at the same time.

> **MODELO** Sandra se baña a las siete y media. Francisco y Javier se quitan la ropa a las ocho. Sandra, Manuel y yo nos acostamos a las nueve de la noche.

¿Sabías que...?

The traditional **siesta** at midday enabled people in warm climates to avoid the hottest temperatures of the day and to stay up late, when temperatures were cooler. Today, the midday nap is becoming increasingly rare.

CONEXIÓN CON LAS MATEMÁTICAS

Estimating Time Keep a journal for three days, noting the times you do things in the morning and at night.

Write the time you wake up in the morning, as well as the times you do different things to get ready for school. You should also write the time you leave for school. Then write the time you return home, and the times you do things to get ready for bed.

Look at Ana's entry for **el lunes:**

> lunes
>
> POR LA MAÑANA
> Primero me despierto a las seis y media.
> Luego me baño a las siete menos cinco.
> Por último, me voy a la escuela a las ocho menos veinte.
> POR LA NOCHE
> Primero vuelvo a casa a las cuatro.
> Luego me pongo el pijama a las nueve.
> Por último me acuesto a las nueve y media.

At the end of three days, compare your journal with a partner's. Estimate how much time you spend doing each activity. How similar are your routines?

En resumen

Me acuesto.	**acostarse**
Me baño.	**bañarse**
Me ducho.	**ducharse**
Me quito la ropa.	**quitarse**
Vuelvo a la casa.	**volver**

¿Cómo se dice?

Talking about closing things

Each day you open and close all sorts of things. You already know how to talk about opening things. The verb "to close" in Spanish is **cerrar.** Here's how to use it.

Singular

Plural

Cierro la puerta.

Cerramos las ventanas.

¿Cierras la puerta del dormitorio?

¿Ustedes **cierran** la puerta?

Él **cierra** la puerta.

Ellos **cierran** la puerta y las ventanas.

Did you notice that in most cases, the **e** changed to **ie?**

Two other useful verbs that change in this way are **pensar,** which means "to think" or "to plan" (when used with another infinitive verb), and **comenzar,** which means "to begin."

Pienso estudiar.

Ellos **comienzan** a nadar ahora.

Singular

	CERRAR	PENSAR	COMENZAR
Yo	c**ie**rro	p**ie**nso	com**ie**nzo
Tú	c**ie**rras	p**ie**nsas	com**ie**nzas
Él, Ella, Ud.	c**ie**rra	p**ie**nsa	com**ie**nza

Plural

Nosotros, Nosotras	cerr**amos**	pens**amos**	comenz**amos**
Ellos, Ellas, Uds.	c**ie**rr**an**	p**ie**ns**an**	com**ie**nz**an**

¡Úsalo!

A Fill out a schedule like this one with the different classes you have every day. Write the time when each class starts.

Hora	lunes	martes	miércoles	jueves	viernes
10:30				arte	

Then get together with a partner. Ask each other questions to see if you filled out your schedule correctly.

MODELO —¿A qué hora comienza la clase de arte el jueves?

—A las diez y media.

B You are writing an essay for your school newspaper about a day in the life of a student. Interview one of your classmates using the list of questions below. Be sure to write down the answers. You can add more questions if you like. Then write a paragraph about your partner's day.

1. ¿A qué hora te despiertas?
2. ¿Cuándo te lavas el pelo?
3. ¿Te bañas por la mañana o por la noche?
4. ¿A qué hora te pones la ropa?
5. ¿A qué hora te vas de casa?
6. ¿A qué hora comienzan tus clases?
7. ¿A qué hora vuelves a casa?
8. ¿A qué hora te acuestas?

C Your room is a mess. Your mother wants to know if you're planning to clean it up.

Partner A: You are the mother. Ask if your child is planning to do each task.

Partner B: Answer according to what needs to be done in the picture.

> **MODELO** —¿Piensas colgar la ropa?
>
> —Sí, pienso colgar la ropa.

colgar la ropa
quitar el polvo
regar las plantas
barrer el piso
pasar la aspiradora
sacar la basura
limpiar las ventanas
cerrar los cajones
recoger las cosas

D Get together with a partner. Read these sentences about different types of weather. Your partner has to tell you whether he or she opens or closes windows and doors in each type of weather.

> **MODELO** —Hace mucho sol.
>
> —Abro las puertas. Abro las ventanas.

Hace calor.
Hace frío.
Nieva.
Llueve.
Hace viento.

CONEXIÓN CON LAS MATEMÁTICAS

Survey Ask eight different classmates when they plan to watch TV this weekend: Friday, Saturday, or Sunday? Indicate the time of day by putting check marks on a chart like this one.

¿Cuándo piensas mirar la televisión este fin de semana?

viernes	sábado	domingo

Then make a bar graph showing the number of students who watch TV on each day.

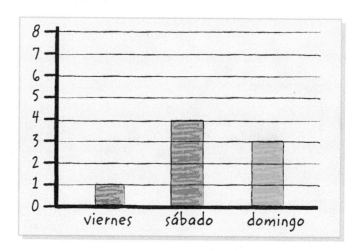

En resumen

	e → ie	e → ie	e → ie
	cerrar	**pensar**	**comenzar**
(Yo)	cierro	pienso	comienzo
(Tú)	cierras	piensas	comienzas
(Él, Ella, Ud.)	cierra	piensa	comienza
(Nosotros, Nosotras)	cerramos	pensamos	comenzamos
(Ellos, Ellas, Uds.)	cierran	piensan	comienzan

¿Cómo se dice?

Talking about doing things for yourself

One of the routine things you do for yourself is get up in the morning. Look at these sentences to see how to use the verb **levantarse.**

Singular	**Plural**

Me levanto a las seis.

Nos levantamos a las siete.

¿A qué hora **te levantas?**

¿A qué hora **se levantan** ustedes?

Él **se levanta** a la salida del sol.

Ellos **se levantan** ahora.

Did you notice the words that came before the different verb forms: **me, te, se,** and **nos?**

These words are called reflexive pronouns. They are always used before verbs with infinitives that end in **-se,** such as **levantarse, bañarse,** and **secarse.**

Singular

	levantarse	**bañarse**	**secarse**
Yo	**me** levanto	**me** baño	**me** seco
Tú	**te** levantas	**te** bañas	**te** secas
Él, Ella, Ud.	**se** levanta	**se** baña	**se** seca

Plural

	levantarse	**bañarse**	**secarse**
Nosotros, Nosotras	**nos** levantamos	**nos** bañamos	**nos** secamos
Ellos, Ellas, Uds.	**se** levantan	**se** bañan	**se** secan

These verbs are called "reflexive verbs." In this unit you have learned other reflexive verbs, too. All reflexive verbs help you to talk about actions you do for yourself, such as brushing your teeth **(cepillarse los dientes),** combing your hair **(peinarse),** and putting on your clothes **(ponerse la ropa).**

Here are some more verbs for very common activities that you know: leaving, going to bed, and waking up (**irse, acostarse, despertarse**).

irse

Singular

Yo	me **voy**
Tú	te **vas**
Él, Ella, Ud.	se **va**

Plural

Nosotros, Nosotras	nos **vamos**
Ellos, Ellas, Uds.	se **van**

acostarse (o ➡ ue)

Singular

Yo	me ac**ue**sto
Tú	te ac**ue**stas
Él, Ella, Ud.	se ac**ue**sta

Plural

Nosotros, Nosotras	nos acostamos
Ellos, Ellas, Uds.	se ac**ue**stan

despertarse (e ➡ ie)

Singular

Yo	me desp**ie**rto
Tú	te desp**ie**rtas
Él, Ella, Ud.	se desp**ie**rta

Plural

Nosotros, Nosotras	nos despertamos
Ellos, Ellas, Uds.	se desp**ie**rtan

¡Úsalo!

A Ask a partner about things that his or her relatives do on weekdays. Make a chart like this one and fill it in with the information your partner gives you.

MODELO —¿A qué hora se levanta tu papá?

—Se levanta a las cinco de la mañana.

	papá	mamá	hermano / hermana
levantarse			
bañarse			
irse			
acostarse			

B Look at these pictures of a typical Sunday at the Álvarez home. Put them in the correct order. Then work with a partner to describe the pictures.

MODELO Los domingos, los Álvarez se levantan a las nueve de la mañana.

1.

2.

3.

4.

5.

6.

7.

8.

CONEXIÓN CON LAS MATEMÁTICAS

Telling Time In many Spanish-speaking countries, people tell time based on a 24-hour clock. After 12:00 p.m., they go on to 13:00 hours instead of 1:00 p. m., 14:00 hours instead of 2:00 p. m., and so on.

Look at these photos of Alba, a girl from Spain. Write the times you see using the usual twelve-hour clock you know. Then describe Alba's day in the right order to a partner.

09:00

08:00

22:00

13:30

En resumen

	levantarse	bañarse	secarse
(Yo)	**me** levant**o**	**me** bañ**o**	**me** sec**o**
(Tú)	**te** levant**as**	**te** bañ**as**	**te** sec**as**
(Él, Ella, Ud.)	**se** levant**a**	**se** bañ**a**	**se** sec**a**
(Nosotros, Nosotras)	**nos** levant**amos**	**nos** bañ**amos**	**nos** sec**amos**
(Ellos, Ellas, Uds.)	**se** levant**an**	**se** bañ**an**	**se** sec**an**

		o ➡ ue	e ➡ ie
	irse	**acostarse**	**despertarse**
(Yo)	me **voy**	**me** ac**ue**sto	**me** desp**ie**rto
(Tú)	te **vas**	**te** ac**ue**stas	**te** desp**ie**rtas
(Él, Ella, Ud.)	se **va**	**se** ac**ue**sta	**se** desp**ie**rta
(Nosotros, Nosotras)	nos **vamos**	**nos** ac**o**stamos	**nos** despert**amos**
(Ellos, Ellas, Uds.)	se **van**	**se** ac**ue**stan	**se** desp**ie**rtan

¿Dónde se habla español?

Caracas

VENEZUELA

Venezuela

When Columbus arrived in Venezuela on his third voyage (1498), more than 300,000 indigenous people were living throughout the country— the Caribs, Arawaks and Chibchas. Now Venezuela is one of South America's richest countries. Oil is its main resource and the base of its economy. Venezuela has many natural wonders such as Angel Falls **(Salto Ángel),** the highest waterfall in the world. It was named for a pilot

from the United States, Jimmie Angel. Further south, in the Amazon basin, you can stay in a thatched hut in dense jungle, at the base of a line of magnificent waterfalls **(Saltos Hacha).** This area is called Canaima. There you can see many species of plants and animals and hike on the trails in the surrounding area. For those who like swimming in the Caribbean and sunning on the beach, Isla Margarita is a popular destination.

Through the southeast you'll see **tepuyes,** which are flat-topped mountains that look almost like a lunar landscape. You can try some of the national dishes like **arepas** (small pancakes stuffed with meat, seafood or lots of other things) or **hallaca** (dough filled with meat and vegetables wrapped in a banana leaf).

Baseball is the most popular sport in Venezuela, followed by basketball. The traditional music is a folk rhythm known as **joropo:** singing or a dance accompanied by harp, **cuatro,** and **maracas.**

Datos

Capital: Caracas

Ciudades importantes: Ciudad Bolívar, Maracaibo, Mérida, Valencia

Idiomas: Español, idiomas indígenas

Moneda: El bolívar

Población: 24.7 millones

¡Léelo en español!

Simón Bolívar (1783–1830)   Simón Bolívar fue[1] el Gran Libertador[2] de América del Sur. Era de raíces venezolanas y criollas.[3] Su familia era rica, pero de niño, sus padres murieron[4] y fue a vivir con su tío. En la escuela Simón era travieso, pero inteligente. Fue a España para estudiar por tres años. Luego fue a París, Francia y estudió las ideas de libertad. Era la época de Napoleón.

Después Simón visitó los Estados Unidos, habló con norteamericanos y volvió a Venezuela en 1807. La gente de Venezuela quería[5] la independencia, pero perdió contra España en su lucha. Simón tuvo que luchar[6] mucho. Fue un líder excepcional. Por fin, Venezuela ganó su independencia de España. Entonces Bolívar viajó a otros países para ayudarlos a ganar su independencia. Ecuador, Bolivia, Perú y Colombia ganaron su independencia de España. Por eso, lo llaman[7] el Gran Libertador.

[1] was   [2] Liberator   [3] creole   [4] died
[5] wanted   [6] had to fight   [7] they call him

Reading Strategy

Using Graphics Using graphics can help you understand a reading. Draw a circle and put the name of the person the reading is about in the middle. Draw lines from the circle and jot down a fact that you learned about him in a circle at the end of each line. Add additional details about the main point on lines going around that circle.

¡Comprendo!

Answer in English.
Make an outline of the reading on Simón Bolívar. Use his name as your title. List the major points. Under each point list any additional details. Here are some questions to get you started:

1. Where and when was Simón Bolívar born?

2. Where was he educated?

3. How did his travels affect his view of the world?

4. How did he become well-known in Latin America?

¿Qué hacen en la escuela?

Objetivos

- To talk about different places in your school
- To identify the people who work in a school
- To talk about what you know how to do
- To compare two or more people and things
- To learn more about schools in Spanish-speaking countries

A girl leaves school for the day in Cuba.

A school in Zacatecas, Mexico

¿Sabías que...?

- It's not that common for schools in Spanish-speaking countries to have their own cafeterias. In fact, in some places, students go home for lunch.

- Students in Spanish-speaking countries usually don't have lockers at school to store their books, coats, and other things. They carry book bags.

- In Puerto Rico, students learn English from an early age. Although they speak Spanish, their textbooks may be in Spanish or in English.

¿Cómo se dice?

¿Quién trabaja en la escuela?

—¿Quién trabaja en la oficina?

—La asistente administrativa trabaja en la oficina.

la oficina

el asistente administrativo

la directora el director

la asistente administrativa

la biblioteca

el bibliotecario

la bibliotecaria

—Tengo que hablar con los cocineros. ¿Dónde están?

—Están en la cafetería. Allá trabajan.

la cafetería

la cocinera

el cocinero

la enfermería

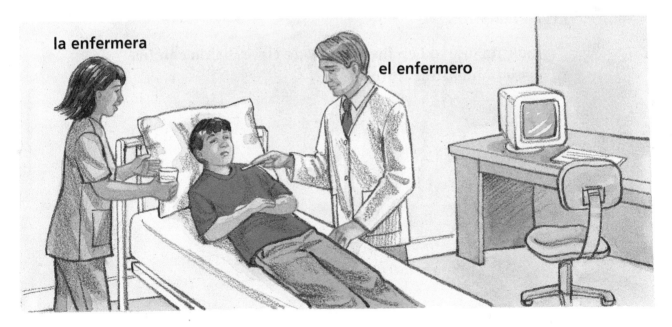

la enfermera

el enfermero

¡Úsalo!

A Work with a partner and write down the names of the different people who work in your school:

> **MODELO** la directora: la Sra. Gómez

If there is a job that doesn't exist in your school, write that down as well.

> **MODELO** No hay (bibliotecario).

When you're finished, compare your list with that of another pair. Did you forget anyone?

B Get together with three or four classmates. Make cards with the job titles of people who work in your school. When your teacher tells you, pick one card and read the job.

In one minute, write as many things as you can about what that person does in school. You're going to play against other teams as your teacher times you. Your team gets one point for every correct verb you use!

> **MODELO** el maestro
>
> **Enseña, trabaja en los salones de clase, habla con los estudiantes, trae libros...**

CONEXIÓN CON LA **SALUD**

Body Temperature Most people have a body temperature around 98.6°F, or 37°C. A higher temperature means that you may have a fever. Body temperatures may change a little during the course of the day—it's usually lower in the morning and higher in the evening.

Does your body temperature change during the day? During the week? Take your temperature twice a day at home and complete a chart like this one. Get together with a partner and make a line graph with your results.

> **MODELO** —¿Qué temperatura tienes el lunes por la mañana?
>
> —Tengo noventa y siete punto dos grados Fahrenheit.

Días	por la mañana	por la noche	¿Tengo fiebre?
lunes	97.2°F		
martes			
miércoles			
jueves			
viernes			
sábado			
domingo			

@ @ @ **Compara** @ @ @

En inglés	**En español**
fever	la fiebre
point	el punto

En resumen

¿Quién **trabaja** en la oficina?	el director	la directora
	el asistente administrativo	la asistente administrativa
en la biblioteca?	el bibliotecario	la bibliotecaria
en la cafetería?	el cocinero	la cocinera
en la enfermería?	el enfermero	la enfermera

¿Cómo se dice?

¿Dónde trabajan en la escuela?

—¿Dónde trabajan los maestros?

—Trabajan en los salones de clase.

los salones de clase

el maestro

la maestra

el pasillo

la fuente de agua

el conserje

la conserje

—¿Hay un auditorio en la escuela?

—Sí, hay un auditorio.

el auditorio

la salida

la entrada

las escaleras

subir las escaleras

bajar las escaleras

Lección 2

doscientos sesenta y uno 261

¡Úsalo!

A On slips of paper, write the jobs of people who work at your school. Then put them in a box. Get together with two classmates. Take turns picking slips of paper out of the box. Your classmates ask questions to guess the job that was picked!

MODELO —¿Trabaja en la cafetería?

—No.

—¿Trabaja en la oficina?

—Sí.

—¿Es la asistente administrativa?

—Sí.

CONEXIÓN CON LA SALUD

Emergency Plan Find the emergency exit route posted in your classroom that shows the way out of your school. Study it to answer questions about different places in school. With a partner, write a bulleted list of instructions for getting out of a certain place and create your own emergency exit route on a school map. When you're done, post it next to the English version.

1. ¿Dónde están las salidas?

2. ¿Qué tienes que hacer primero?

3. ¿Y luego, qué tienes que hacer?

4. ¿Y por último?

B Complete these lines of poetry with nouns from the list that make sense together. Your partner uses the same noun to start the next line. Continue doing one line each, to complete two five-line poems. Use other words if you wish.

En Roma hay una calle,

en la calle hay _____ ,

en _____ hay _____ ,

en _____ hay _____ ,

en _____ hay _____ .

una plaza	*una escuela*	*un salón de clase*
un maestro	*un pasillo*	*un conserje*
un reloj	*un cocinero*	*una cocina*
una biblioteca	*una mesa*	

C Your partner is new at school and doesn't know where to go or how to get to places. Help your partner out by telling him or her where to go and whether he or she has to go up or down the stairs.

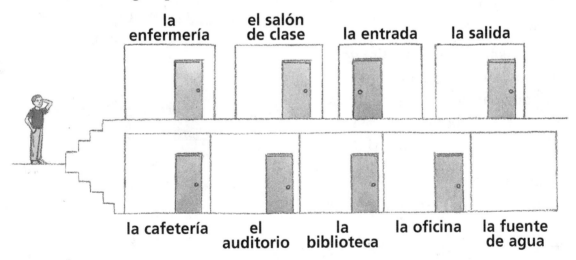

la enfermería   el salón de clase   la entrada   la salida

la cafetería   el auditorio   la biblioteca   la oficina   la fuente de agua

MODELO —Estoy muy mal y me duele la cabeza.

—Tienes que ir a la enfermería. Tienes que subir las escaleras.

1. Tengo mucha hambre.
2. Tengo que hablar con el bibliotecario.
3. Tengo sed.
4. Tengo que usar el teléfono.
5. Tengo que hablar con el maestro.
6. Tengo que ir a casa.

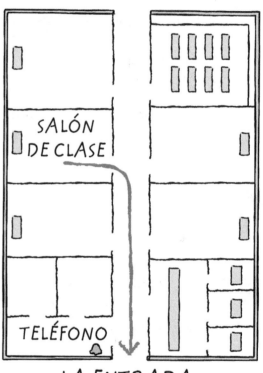

Entre amigos

Draw a map of your school. Label the places you know, including your classroom. Then make cards with these activities.

lavarse las manos
beber agua
volver a casa
usar la computadora
nadar
estudiar
pintar y dibujar
almorzar
usar el teléfono
hablar con el bibliotecario
practicar deportes

Mix up the cards and pick one. Your partner asks you what you're going to do. You answer according to the card. Your partner draws the route from your classroom to the place you need to go. Is your partner right?

—**¿Qué vas a hacer?**

—**Voy a usar el teléfono.**

After picking all the cards and "going" to all the places, switch roles with your partner.

En resumen

bajar las escaleras
subir las escaleras

el auditorio
el conserje

la conserje
la entrada
la fuente de agua
la salida
las escaleras

¿Cómo se dice?

Talking about what you know how to do

You know how to do lots of things. In Spanish, you use the verb **saber** to talk about what you know and what you know how to do. These sentences show you how to use it.

Singular

Yo **sé** cocinar.

¿No **sabes** patinar?

Él no **sabe** peinarse.

Plural

Sabemos nadar muy bien.

¿Uds. no **saben** pintar?

Ellos **saben** bailar.

To talk about knowing how to do something, use one of the forms of **saber** plus an action verb.

¡Úsalo!

A You want to earn some extra allowance. To convince your parents to give it to you, you need to make a list of the things you know how to do around the house. Write a list and then share it with a partner.

MODELO Sé recoger los platos.

CONEXIÓN CON LAS MATEMÁTICAS

Fractions Take a survey in class. Ask each person if he or she knows how to do five different things. Choose your own activities and make a chart like this one.

With a partner, find the fraction of the class that knows how to do each thing, and the fraction that doesn't. Reduce fractions to their simplest terms.

	Saben	No saben
bailar	$\frac{5}{35} = \frac{1}{7}$	$\frac{30}{35} = \frac{6}{7}$
usar la computadora		
cantar bien		
hacer un huevo frito		
dibujar muy bien		

Then share your findings with the class.

MODELO —Pocos alumnos saben bailar.
Muchos alumnos saben...

B Write a list of things you know how to do and things that you don't know how to do. Think of all kinds of things!

Get together with five or six classmates and compare your lists. What things do some of you not know how to do and would like to learn? Write sentences about these activities and share them with the class. How will you learn to do these things?

Sé hacer:	No sé hacer:
1. Sé nadar muy bien.	1. No sé bailar.
2. Sé patinar.	2. No sé planchar la ropa.

MODELO —No sé cocinar pescado.

—Yo tampoco.

—Queremos aprender a cocinar pescado. Vamos a ir a una clase.

C Who knows what? Your teacher will divide the class into pairs, groups, and single students. Each student or group will get a card with an activity.

The game begins when your teacher asks a question. For example, **¿Quién sabe nadar?** The student or group with the card for **nadar** has to say that they know how to do it. See how fast you can answer!

Write a letter to a family in a Spanish-speaking country. You will stay with them this summer as an exchange student.

List some of the things you know how to do. Then list some things you don't know how to do. Look at the letter that Javier wrote:

el 3 de abril

Querida familia en Madrid:
Me llamo Javier Suárez.
Tengo nueve años. Me gusta

mucho hablar español.
Estudio en la escuela
Jefferson. Quiero ir a

España. Sé cocinar muy bien.
No sé practicar deportes ...

Un saludo,
Javier

En resumen

	saber
(Yo)	sé
(Tú)	sabes
(Él, Ella, Ud.)	sabe
(Nosotros, Nosotras)	sabemos
(Ellos, Ellas, Uds.)	saben

¿Cómo se dice?

Making comparisons

Here is how you can compare people and things:

Inés es alta.

Dolores es
más alta que Inés.

Rita es **la más alta.**

Paco es atlético.

David es
más atlético que Paco.

Saúl es **el más atlético.**

You've already practiced comparing two people in an earlier unit. How do you say that one person is "more . . ." than the other?

To say that someone is "the most . . . ," you use **la más** or **el más** followed by a descriptive word. You use the same words to compare more than two things.

La clase de arte es **más** fácil **que** la clase de ciencias.
La clase de español es **la más** fácil **de** todas las clases.

El libro de Iris es **el más** pequeño **de** todos.

CONEXIÓN CON LOS ESTUDIOS SOCIALES

States Get together with four classmates. Work with this map of the United States to compare the different states. Take turns making comparisons. Make sure not to repeat one that has already been made! Whoever makes a wrong comparison, or repeats one, is out of the game. The winner is the last one to remain.

MODELO **Connecticut es más largo que Rhode Island.**

@ @ @ **Compara** @ @ @

En inglés	En español
populated	poblado(a)
inhabitants	los habitantes

¡Úsalo!

A Look at the pictures. Ask questions about these people.

Inés

Marta

Ramón

Marcos

Partner A: Ask a question comparing two of these people.

Partner B: Look at the picture and answer.

> **MODELO** —¿Es Marcos más alto que Inés?
>
> —No, Inés es más alta que Marcos.

CONEXIÓN CON LAS CIENCIAS

◎◎◎ Compara ◎◎◎	
En inglés	**En español**
distance	la distancia
diameter	el diámetro

Solar System Look at these facts. With a partner, compare Jupiter, Uranus, and Earth **(la Tierra).** (Use **caliente** for "hot.") Write as many sentences as you can!

	Júpiter	**Urano**
Distancia del Sol	778,570,010 kilómetros (484,000,000 millas)	2,872,460,200 kilómetros (1,785,000,000 millas)
Diámetro	142,984 kilómetros (88,846 millas)	51,118 kilómetros (31,763 millas)
Un día	10 horas	18 horas
Un año	12 años de la Tierra	84 años de la Tierra
Temperatura	–110° C (–166° F)	–197° C (–323° F)

B Talk with a partner about famous people you know (real and fictional). Make a comparison by using **el más...** or **la más...**

Partner A: Choose a descriptive word to talk about a celebrity using **el más** or **la más.**

Partner B: Use the same descriptive word to talk about another person.

MODELO —Supermán es el más fuerte de todos.

—Michael Jordan es más atlético que David Letterman.

inteligente	fuerte	cómico(a)	tímido(a)	impaciente
alto(a)	atlético(a)	simpático(a)	generoso(a)	popular

Each partner has to talk about five different people.

Entre amigos

Go around your class and ask your classmates who they think has the most of each of these qualities.

—¿Quién es el más fuerte de la clase?
—Adolfo es el más fuerte.

inteligente	generoso(a)	atlético(a)	fuerte	cómico(a)	simpático(a)
			Adolfo		

Then get together with five or six classmates and say who is the winner in each column.

¡El alumno más inteligente de la clase es... !

CONEXIÓN CON EL ARTE

Making Cards Get together with a partner. Pick three people who work in your school, and write each of them a thank-you card for their help during the school year. Decorate the cards using paint, crayons, photos, or the computer as a drawing tool.

Carla and Alberto picked the school nurse. Read what their card says:

Querida Sra. Muñoz:
Eres la más simpática
de todas las enfermeras.

¡Hasta el próximo año!

Carla y Alberto

Deliver the cards to the people you picked. Explain your note to them if they can't read Spanish and be sure to tell them . . .

¡Hasta el próximo año!

See you next year!

En resumen

David es **más** atlético **que** Paco.	Dolores es **más** alta **que** Inés.
Saúl es **el más** atlético **de** todos.	Rita es **la más** alta **de** todas.

¿Dónde se habla español?
Los mexicano-americanos en los Estados Unidos

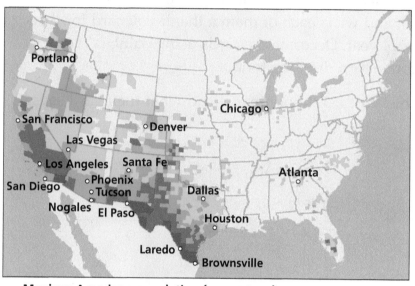

Mexican American population (percentage)

- 50 – 85.8
- 26 – 50
- 13 – 1.4
- 4 – 13
- Less than 4

Much of the United States today was part of Mexico until 1848. The impact and contributions of Mexican Americans have been important in the history of our country. Mexican Americans have lived in the South-

west for generations. Through the years, thousands of Chicanos, or Mexican Americans, (also self-called **tejanos** or **mestizos**) were brought in to many states of the United States as **braceros** (helping hands) to help farmers harvest their crops. They lived in very difficult conditions—poor housing, low wages, no education or health care. They also suffered discrimination. They were supposed to return to Mexico, but many stayed. These Chicanos were often deported. Finally, in the 1940s court cases began defending the rights of Mexican Americans.

In the 1960s and 1970s César Chávez organized the United Farm Workers, a union, which won many rights for farm workers across the country.

Mexican Americans have played major roles in government, education, the media, the arts, and other professions. Hispanics are now the largest minority in the United States.

◎ ◎ ◎ ◎ Datos ◎ ◎ ◎ ◎

Mexican Americans are an important and growing minority in the United States. Nearly 13.5 million U.S. citizens described themselves as Mexican Americans in the 1990 census. They make up the largest group of Hispanic Americans. About four out of five Mexican Americans live in the major cities of the West and Southwest.

¡Léelo en español!

Famosas latinas de ascendencia mexicana En la música contemporánea de los Estados Unidos, muchas latinas de ascendencia[1] mexicana han dejado su huella.[2] Éstas son algunas.

Selena Probablemente Selena fue la primera en preparar el camino[3] para las latinas en la música contemporánea de los Estados Unidos. Ella muestra[4] la mezcla[5] de dos culturas y sus canciones son populares aún hoy día. Su trágica muerte es una pérdida para el mundo.

Thalia Thalia es una actriz muy conocida[6] en las telenovelas[7] como *María*. Una canción de su primer álbum en inglés se llama *I Want You*. Canta con Fat Joe, un rapero. También Thalia empieza una línea de ropa y artículos del hogar[8].

Otras cantantes Jennifer Peña es de San Antonio. Selena es su inspiración. Ella canta al estilo tejano. Tiene dos nominaciones para Grammys. Julieta Venegas es una roquera mexicana. Es de Tijuana, México. Las letras[9] de sus canciones son bonitas. Lila Downs es cantante también. Su mamá es mixteca y su papá es escocés americano. Canta en inglés, español y lenguas indígenas como mixteca, maya y náhuatl. Se viste con trajes tradicionales. Un año en los premios Oscar, cantó[10] la canción *Burn It Blue* de la película *Frida*. Todas estas mujeres están muy orgullosas[11] de su herencia mexicana.

[1] descent   [2] left their mark   [3] pave the way
[4] shows   [5] mixture   [6] well-known
[7] soap operas   [8] home   [9] lyrics   [10] she sang
[11] proud

Reading Strategy

Skimming Skim the reading quickly. Notice any names that are mentioned and make a list of them. As you read the article, list something you learn about each person next to her name.

Recognizing Cognates What do you think these words mean: **contemporánea, trágica, álbum, rapero, nominaciones, roquera?** Use the cognates to help you understand what is being said about these famous Latinas.

¡Comprendo!

Answer in English.
List at least two things you learned about each Mexican American singer. This will help you remember the person better. They are: Selena, Thalia, Jennifer Peña, Julieta Venegas, and Lila Downs.

Appendix

Verbs

Regular Verbs

–ar **Verbs: Model** cocinar

Singular		Plural	
Yo	cocino	Nosotros / Nosotras	cocinamos
Tú	cocinas	Vosotros / Vosotras	cocináis
Él / Ella / Ud.	cocina	Ellos / Ellas / Uds.	cocinan
Present participle: cocinando		Familiar command: ¡Cocina!	

–er **Verbs: Model** comer

Singular		Plural	
Yo	como	Nosotros / Nosotras	comemos
Tú	comes	Vosotros / Vosotras	coméis
Él / Ella / Ud.	come	Ellos / Ellas / Uds.	comen
Present participle: comiendo		Familiar command: ¡Come!	

–ir **Verbs: Model** abrir

Singular		Plural	
Yo	abro	Nosotros / Nosotras	abrimos
Tú	abres	Vosotros / Vosotras	abrís
Él / Ella / Ud.	abre	Ellos / Ellas / Uds.	abren
Present participle: abriendo		Familiar command: ¡Abre!	

Stem-Changing Verbs

o to ue: Model almorzar

Singular		Plural	
Yo	almuerzo	Nosotros / Nosotras	almorzamos
Tú	almuerzas	Vosotros / Vosotras	almorzáis
Él / Ella / Ud.	almuerza	Ellos / Ellas / Uds.	almuerzan
Present participle: almorzando		Familiar command: ¡Almuerza!	

e to ie: Model cerrar

Singular		Plural	
Yo	cierro	Nosotros / Nosotras	cerramos
Tú	cierras	Vosotros / Vosotras	cerráis
Él / Ella / Ud.	cierra	Ellos / Ellas / Uds.	cierran
Present participle: cerrando		Familiar command: ¡Cierra!	

Irregular Verbs

estar

Singular		Plural	
Yo	estoy	Nosotros / Nosotras	estamos
Tú	estás	Vosotros / Vosotras	estáis
Él / Ella / Ud.	está	Ellos / Ellas / Uds.	están

ir

Singular		Plural	
Yo	voy	Nosotros / Nosotras	vamos
Tú	vas	Vosotros / Vosotras	vais
Él / Ella / Ud.	va	Ellos / Ellas / Uds.	van

poner

Singular		Plural	
Yo	pongo	Nosotros / Nosotras	ponemos
Tú	pones	Vosotros / Vosotras	ponéis
Él / Ella / Ud.	pone	Ellos / Ellas / Uds.	ponen

saber

Singular		Plural	
Yo	sé	Nosotros / Nosotras	sabemos
Tú	sabes	Vosotros / Vosotras	sabéis
Él / Ella / Ud.	sabe	Ellos / Ellas / Uds.	saben

ser

Singular		Plural	
Yo	soy	Nosotros / Nosotras	somos
Tú	eres	Vosotros / Vosotras	sois
Él / Ella / Ud.	es	Ellos / Ellas / Uds.	son

tener

Singular		Plural	
Yo	tengo	Nosotros / Nosotras	tenemos
Tú	tienes	Vosotros / Vosotras	tenéis
Él / Ella / Ud.	tiene	Ellos / Ellas / Uds.	tienen

traer

Singular		Plural	
Yo	traigo	Nosotros / Nosotras	traemos
Tú	traes	Vosotros / Vosotras	traéis
Él / Ella / Ud.	trae	Ellos / Ellas / Uds.	traen

Reflexive Verbs

Model levantarse

Singular		Plural	
Yo	me levanto	Nosotros / Nosotras	nos levantamos
Tú	te levantas	Vosotros / Vosotras	os levantáis
Él / Ella / Ud.	se levanta	Ellos / Ellas / Uds.	se levantan

Many verbs can become reflexive by adding *me, te, se, nos*, and *os* to the appropiate verb forms.

Numbers

0 cero	**26** veintiséis	**51** cincuenta y uno	**76** setenta y seis
1 uno	**27** veintisiete	**52** cincuenta y dos	**77** setenta y siete
2 dos	**28** veintiocho	**53** cincuenta y tres	**78** setenta y ocho
3 tres	**29** veintinueve	**54** cincuenta y cuatro	**79** setenta y nueve
4 cuatro	**30** treinta	**55** cincuenta y cinco	**80** ochenta
5 cinco	**31** treinta y uno	**56** cincuenta y seis	**81** ochenta y uno
6 seis	**32** treinta y dos	**57** cincuenta y siete	**82** ochenta y dos
7 siete	**33** treinta y tres	**58** cincuenta y ocho	**83** ochenta y tres
8 ocho	**34** treinta y cuatro	**59** cincuenta y nueve	**84** ochenta y cuatro
9 nueve	**35** treinta y cinco	**60** sesenta	**85** ochenta y cinco
10 diez	**36** treinta y seis	**61** sesenta y uno	**86** ochenta y seis
11 once	**37** treinta y siete	**62** sesenta y dos	**87** ochenta y siete
12 doce	**38** treinta y ocho	**63** sesenta y tres	**88** ochenta y ocho
13 trece	**39** treinta y nueve	**64** sesenta y cuatro	**89** ochenta y nueve
14 catorce	**40** cuarenta	**65** sesenta y cinco	**90** noventa
15 quince	**41** cuarenta y uno	**66** sesenta y seis	**91** noventa y uno
16 dieciséis	**42** cuarenta y dos	**67** sesenta y siete	**92** noventa y dos
17 diecisiete	**43** cuarenta y tres	**68** sesenta y ocho	**93** noventa y tres
18 dieciocho	**44** cuarenta y cuatro	**69** sesenta y nueve	**94** noventa y cuatro
19 diecinueve	**45** cuarenta y cinco	**70** setenta	**95** noventa y cinco
20 veinte	**46** cuarenta y seis	**71** setenta y uno	**96** noventa y seis
21 veintiuno	**47** cuarenta y siete	**72** setenta y dos	**97** noventa y siete
22 veintidós	**48** cuarenta y ocho	**73** setenta y tres	**98** noventa y ocho
23 veintitrés	**49** cuarenta y nueve	**74** setenta y cuatro	**99** noventa y nueve
24 veinticuatro	**50** cincuenta	**75** setenta y cinco	**100** cien
25 veinticinco			

Hay doscientos alumnos en la escuela.
Hay trescientas sillas en el auditorio.
Hay cuatrocientas cincuenta uvas en la caja.
Hay quinientos pájaros en el parque.
Hay seiscientos libros en mi biblioteca.
Hay setecientas alumnas en la escuela.
Hay ochocientas computadoras en las oficinas.
Hay novecientos veinticinco bolígrafos.
Hay mil quinientas cerezas en la mesa.

Countries and Nationalities

Países donde se habla español	La gente
(la) **Argentina**	el argentino, la argentina
Bolivia	el boliviano, la boliviana
Chile	el chileno, la chilena
Colombia	el colombiano, la colombiana
Costa Rica	el costarricense, la costarricense
Cuba	el cubano, la cubana
(el) **Ecuador**	el ecuatoriano, la ecuatoriana
El Salvador	el salvadoreño, la salvadoreña
España	el español, la española
(los) **Estados Unidos**	el estadounidense, la estadounidense
Guatemala	el guatemalteco, la guatemalteca
(la) **Guinea Ecuatorial**	el guineo, la guinea
Honduras	el hondureño, la hondureña
México	el mexicano, la mexicana
Nicaragua	el nicaragüense, la nicaragüense
Panamá	el panameño, la panameña
(el) **Paraguay**	el paraguayo, la paraguaya
(el) **Perú**	el peruano, la peruana
Puerto Rico (Estado Libre Asociado/commonwealth)	el puertorriqueño, la puertorriqueña
(la) **República Dominicana**	el dominicano, la dominicana
(el) **Uruguay**	el uruguayo, la uruguaya
Venezuela	el venezolano, la venezolana

Los continentes	La gente
(el) **África**	el africano, la africana
América del Norte	el norteamericano, la norteamericana
América del Sur	el sudamericano, la sudamericana
Antártida	—-
Asia	el asiático, la asiática
Australia	el australiano, la australiana
Europa	el europeo, la europea

Otros países	La gente
Alemania	el alemán, la alemana
Belice	el beliceño, la beliceña
(el) **Brasil**	el brasileño, la brasileña
(el) **Canadá**	el canadiense, la canadiense
China	el chino, la china
Egipto	el egipcio, la egipcia
Francia	el francés, la francesa
Grecia	el griego, la griega
Haití	el haitiano, la haitiana
Inglaterra	el inglés, la inglesa
Irlanda	el irlandés, la irlandesa
Italia	el italiano, la italiana
Jamaica	el jamaiquino, la jamaiquina
Japón	el japonés, la japonesa
Marruecos	el marroquí, la marroquí
Nigeria	el nigeriano, la nigeriana
Portugal	el portugués, la portuguesa
Rusia	el ruso, la rusa
Turquía	el turco, la turca

Word List

Spanish-English

The Spanish-English Word List contains the Spanish words you've already learned in *¡Hola!* and the words you learn in each unit of *¿Qué tal?* A number in parentheses indicates the unit where a word was taught. (H) indicates that a word comes from *¡Hola!*

Here's a sample entry—a word and its English equivalent:

la **computadora**   computer   (H)

The bold letters in different type tell you that **computadora** is the entry. "La" tells you to use "la," (not "el") with **computadora.** (H) tells you that **computadora** first appears in one of the units of *¡Hola!*

Here's another entry:

el **refrigerador**   (*pl.: refrigeradores*)   refrigerator (6)

The abbreviation *pl. (plural)* in parentheses tells you that **refrigeradores** is the word you use for more than one. (6) tells you that **refrigerador** is taught in **Unidad 6** of *¿Qué tal?*

Here are the complete Word List abbreviations:

Abbreviations

adj.	adjective	*inf.*	infinitive
adv.	adverb	*m.*	masculine
com.	command	*pl.*	plural
f.	feminine	*s.*	singular

A

a to, at (H)

¿A qué hora? At what time? (H)

a veces sometimes (H)

el **abrelatas** (*pl.: los abrelatas*) can opener (6)

el **abrigo** coat (2)

abril April (H)

abrir to open (6)

la **abuela** grandmother (H)

el **abuelo** grandfather (H)

los **abuelos** grandparents (H)

aburrido, aburrida boring (H)

acabar to finish, to just finish (7)

acabar de (*+ inf.*) to have just (done something) (7)

acostarse (o ➡ ue) (*reflexive*) to go to bed (11)

adiós good-bye (H)

¿Adónde? (to) Where? (H)

agosto August (H)

el **agua** (*f.*) water (9)

ahora now (H)

al (*a + el*) to the (H)

las **albóndigas** meatballs (10)

la **alfombra** rug, carpet (5)

la **almohada** pillow (5)

almorzar (o ➡ ue) to eat (have) lunch (10)

el **almuerzo** lunch (10)

alto, alta tall (H)

la **alumna** (female) student (H)

el **alumno** (male) student (H)

amarillo, amarilla yellow (H)

la **amiga** (female) friend (H)

el **amigo** (male) friend (H)

los **amigos** (male or male and female) friends (H)

anaranjado, anaranjada orange (color) (H)

el **animal** (*pl.: animales*) animal (H)

antes before (7)

antipático, antipática unpleasant (H)

el **año** year (H)

¿Cuántos años tiene? How old is he (she)? (H)

los meses del año the months of the year (H)

el **apartamento** apartment (4)

aprender to learn (H)

aprender a + inf. to learn (how to do something) (H)

el **arroz** rice (10)

el **arte** (*m.*) art (H)

así so (H)

así, así so-so (H)

la **asistente administrativa** (female) administrative assistant (12)

el **asistente administrativo** (male) administrative assistant (12)

la **aspiradora** vacuum cleaner (7)

pasar la aspiradora to vacuum (7)

el **ático** attic (4)

atlético, atlética athletic (3)

el **auditorio** auditorium (12)

la **avena** oatmeal (9)

¡Ay! Oh!, Ouch! (H)

el **azúcar** sugar (8)

azul blue (H)

B

bailar to dance (H)

bajar to go down (12)

bajar las escaleras to go down the stairs (12)

bajo, baja short (H)

el **balcón** (*pl.: balcones*) balcony (4)

la **bandera** flag (H)

bañarse (*reflexive*) to take a bath (11)

el traje de baño bathing suit, swimsuit (2)

barrer to sweep (7)

barrer el piso to sweep the floor (7)

la **basura** trash (7)

sacar la basura to take out the trash (7)

la **bata** robe, bathrobe (2)

la **batidora eléctrica** electric mixer (6)

batir to beat, to whisk (food) (6)

beber to drink (9)

la **biblioteca** library (H)

la **bibliotecaria** (female) librarian (12)

el **bibliotecario** (male) librarian (12)

bien well, fine (H)

Me queda bien. It fits me well. (2)

muy bien very well (H)

¡Bienvenidos! Welcome! (H)

la **bisabuela** great-grandmother (H)

el **bisabuelo** great-grandfather (H)

los **bisabuelos** great-grandparents (H)

blanco, blanca white (H)

la **blusa** blouse (2)

la **boca** mouth (1)

el **bol** (*pl.: boles*) bowl (6)

el **bolígrafo** ballpoint pen (H)

la **bombilla** light bulb (6)

bonito, bonita pretty (2)

el **borrador** (*pl.: borradores*) chalk eraser (H)

las **botas** boots (2)

el **brazo** arm (1)

buen good (*before a m. s. noun*) (H)

Hace buen tiempo.
The weather is good. (H)

bueno, buena good (H)

¡Buenas noches! Good evening!, Good night! (H)

¡Buenas tardes!
Good afternoon! (H)

¡Buenos días!
Good morning! (H)

el **buzón** (*pl.: buzones*) mailbox (4)

C

la **cabeza** head (1)

el **café** coffee (9)

la **cafetería** cafeteria (12)

la **caja** box (6)

el **cajón** (*pl.: cajones*) drawer (6)

el **calcetín** (*pl.: calcetines*) socks, knee socks (2)

el **calendario** calendar (H)

el **calor** heat (H)

Hace calor. It's hot. (H)

Tengo calor. I'm hot. (H)

la **cama** bed (5)

caminar to walk (H)

la **camisa** shirt (2)

la **camiseta** T-shirt, polo shirt, undershirt (2)

el **canario** canary (H)

canoso, canosa gray (hair) (3)

cantar to sing (H)

la **cara** face (1)

la **carne** meat (10)

el **cartel** (*pl.: carteles*) poster (5)

la **casa** house, home (H)

castaño, castaña brown, chestnut (hair) (3)

la **ceja** eyebrow (1)

celebrar to celebrate (H)

la **cena** dinner (10)

cenar to have dinner (10)

cepillarse (*reflexive*) to brush oneself (11)

cepillarse los dientes (*reflexive*) to brush one's teeth (11)

la **cerca** fence (4)

cerca de near, close to (5)

el **cereal** cereal (9)

la **cereza** cherry (8)

cerrar (e ➜ ie) to close, to shut (11)

la **chaqueta** jacket (2)

la **chica** girl (H)

el **chico** boy (H)

la **chimenea** fireplace, chimney (4)

el **chocolate** chocolate (9)

    el chocolate caliente hot chocolate (9)

las **ciencias** science (H)

el **cine** movie theater, movies (H)

    ir al cine to go to the movies (H)

la **cintura** waist (1)

el **círculo** circle (H)

    claro *(adv.)* of course (H)

    ¡Claro que sí! Of course! (H)

la **clase** class (H)

    la clase de computadoras computer class (H)

    el salón de clase classroom (H)

la **cocina** kitchen (4)

    cocinar to cook (6)

la **cocinera** (female) cook (12)

el **cocinero** (male) cook (12)

el **codo** elbow (1)

    colgar (o ➡ ue) to hang up (7)

    colgar la ropa to hang up clothes (7)

el **color** *(pl.: colores)* color (H)

    ¿De qué color es? What color is it? (H)

el **comedor** dining room, (school) cafeteria (4)

    comenzar (e ➡ ie) to begin, to start (11)

    comer to eat (6)

    cómico, cómica funny, amusing (3)

la **comida** food (10)

    ¿Cómo...? How...? What...? (H)

    ¿Cómo es...? What is … like? (H)

    ¿Cómo me queda? How does it fit me? (2)

    ¿Cómo se dice? How do you say it? (H)

    comprar to buy (H)

    comprender to understand (H)

la **computadora** computer (H)

    la clase de computadoras computer class (H)

    usar la computadora to use the computer (H)

    con with (7)

el **conejo** rabbit (H)

    conexión connection (H)

el **conserje** (male) custodian (12)

la **conserje** (female) custodian (12)

    correr to run (6)

las **cortinas** curtains (5)

    corto, corta short (H)

la **crema** cream (8)

    la crema de cacahuate peanut butter (10)

el **cuaderno** notebook (H)

el **cuadrado** square (H)

el **cuadro** painting (5)

    ¿Cuál? *(pl.: Cuáles)* What?, Which one(s)? (H)

    ¿Cuál es tu número de teléfono? What is your telephone number? (H)

    ¿Cuándo? When? (H)

    ¿Cuánto? *(m. s.)*, **¿Cuánta?** *(f. s.)* How much? (H)

    ¿Cuánto es... más...? How much is… plus… ? (H)

    ¿Cuántos? *(m. pl.)*, **¿Cuántas?** *(f. pl.)* How many? (H)

    ¿Cuántos/Cuántas... hay? How many… are there? (H)

    ¿Cuántos años tienes? How old are you? (H)

el **cuarto** quarter (H); room (4)

    un cuarto de hora a quarter of an hour (H)

    una hora y cuarto an hour and a quarter (H)

el **cuarto de baño** bathroom (4)

la **cuchara** spoon, tablespoon (8)

la **cucharita** teaspoon (8)

el **cuchillo** knife (8)

el **cuello** neck (1)

el **cuerpo** body (1)

    las partes del cuerpo parts of the body (1)

el **cumpleaños** birthday (H)

    ¿Cuándo es tu cumpleaños? When is your birthday? (H)

    ¡Feliz cumpleaños! Happy birthday! (H)

D

    de of, in, from (H)

    ¿De quién? Whose? (H)

    cerca de near, close to (5)

    debajo de under, underneath (8)

    débil weak (3)

el **dedo** finger (1)

    del (*de + el*) of the (2), from the (5)

    delante de in front of (5)

    dentro de inside, in (4)

los **deportes** sports (H)

    practicar deportes to practice (play) sports (H)

el **desayuno** breakfast (9)

el **despacho** study, office (4)

    despertarse (**e ➡ ie**) (*reflexive*) to wake up (11)

    detrás de behind, in back of (5)

el **día** day (H)

    el día de la semana weekday (H)

    el día de fiesta holiday (H)

    dibujar to draw (H)

    diciembre December (H)

el **diente** tooth (1)

    difícil (*pl.: difíciles*) difficult (H)

el **director** (male) director, school principal (12)

la **directora** (female) director, school principal (12)

divertido, divertida amusing, entertaining, fun (H)

doler (**o ➡ ue**) to hurt, to ache (1)

    Me duele la cabeza. My head hurts. I have a headache. (1)

    Le duele el pie. His/her foot hurts. (1)

    Le duelen los pies. His/her feet hurt. (1)

    Te duele el brazo. Your arm hurts. (1)

el **domingo** Sunday (H)

    los domingos on Sundays (H)

¿dónde? where? (H)

el **dormitorio** bedroom (4)

ducharse (*reflexive*) to take a shower (11)

el **durazno** peach (8)

el **DVD** DVD (disc) (5)

E

el **ecuador** equator (H)

la **educación física** physical education (H)

el (*m. s.*) the (H)

él he (H)

eléctrico, eléctrica electric, electrical (6)

    la batidora eléctrica electric mixer (6)

ella she (H)

ellas (*f.*) they (4)

ellos (*m.*) they (4)

en in, on (H)

    en punto on the dot, sharp (time) (H)

el **enchufe** plug, electrical socket (6)

enero January (H)

la **enfermera** (female) nurse (12)

la **enfermería** infirmary, nurse's office (12)

el **enfermero** (male) nurse (12)

la **ensalada** salad (10)

la **entrada** entrance (12)

entre among, between (H)

entre amigos among friends (H)

Es... It's... (H)

las **escaleras** stairs (4)

bajar las escaleras to go down the stairs (12)

subir las escaleras to go up the stairs (12)

la **escoba** broom (7)

escribir to write (H)

el **escritorio** teacher's desk (H)

escuchar to listen (H)

la **escuela** school (H)

los **espaguetis** spaghetti (10)

los espaguetis con albóndigas spaghetti with meatballs (10)

la **espalda** back (1)

el **español** Spanish (H)

espectacular spectacular (H)

el **espejo** mirror (5)

la **estación** season (H)

el **estante** shelf (5)

la **estantería** bookcase (5)

estar to be (H)

Está lloviendo. It's raining. (H)

Está nevando. It's snowing. (H)

Está nublado. It's cloudy. (H)

estás you (*familiar*) are (H)

Estoy muy mal. I don't feel well at all. (H)

el **estéreo** sound system, stereo (5)

estudiar to study (H)

los **estudios sociales** social studies (H)

la **estufa** stove (6)

F

fabuloso, fabulosa fabulous (H)

fácil (*pl.: fáciles*) easy (H)

la **falda** skirt (2)

la **familia** family (H)

fantástico, fantástica fantastic (H)

el **favor** favor (9)

por favor please (9)

favorito, favorita favorite (H)

febrero February (H)

la **fecha** date (H)

¿Qué fecha es hoy? What's today's date? (H)

feliz (*pl.: felices*) happy (H)

¡Feliz cumpleaños! Happy birthday!

feo, fea ugly (2)

el **fin** (*pl.: fines*) end (H)

el fin de semana weekend (H)

flaco, flaca thin (H)

el **flamenco** flamingo (H)

el **fregadero** sink (6)

la **frente** forehead (1)

la **fresa** strawberry (8)

fresco, fresca cool, fresh (H)

Hace fresco. It's cool (weather). (H)

los **frijoles** beans (10)

frío, fría cold (H)

Hace frío. It's cold (weather). (H)

tener frío to be cold (H)

frito, frita fried (9)

la **fruta** fruit (8)

la **fuente de agua** drinking fountain, water fountain (12)

fuera de out, outside (4)

fuerte strong (3)

G

el **gabinete** cabinet (6)

el **garaje** garage (4)

el **gato** cat (H)

generoso, generosa generous (3)

el **gimnasio** gymnasium (H)

el **globo** globe (H)

gordo, gorda fat (H)

la **gorra** cap (2)

gracias thank you (H)

grande big, large (H)

el **grifo** faucet (6)

la **gripe** flu (H)

    tener la gripe to have the flu (H)

gris gray (H)

guapo, guapa good-looking (H)

el **guisante** pea (10)

gustar to like, to please (H)

    ¿Qué te gusta hacer...? What do you like to do...? (H)

    Le gusta el verano. He/She likes summer. (H)

    Me gusta la primavera. I like spring. (H)

    ¿Te gusta pintar? Do you like to paint? (H)

H

hablar to speak, to talk (H)

hacer to do, to make (H)

    Hace frío. It's cold. (H)

    Hace sol. It's sunny. (H)

    ¿Qué tiempo hace? What's the weather like? (H)

    ¿Qué vas a hacer? What are you going to do? (H)

el **hambre** (*f.*) hunger (H)

    tener hambre to be hungry (H)

la **hamburguesa** hamburger (10)

hasta until (H)

    ¡Hasta luego! See you later! (H)

    ¡Hasta mañana! See you tomorrow! (H)

    ¡Hasta pronto! See you soon! (H)

hay there is, there are (H)

el **helado** ice cream (10)

la **hermana** sister (H)

la **hermanastra** stepsister (H)

el **hermanastro** stepbrother (H)

el **hermano** brother (H)

los **hermanos** brothers and sisters, brothers (H)

la **hija** daughter (H)

el **hijo** son (H)

los **hijos** children, sons and daughters (H)

la **hoja de papel** sheet of paper (H)

¡Hola! Hello!, Hi! (H)

el **hombre** man (H)

el **hombro** shoulder (1)

la **hora** hour, time (H)

    ¿A qué hora...? At what time...? (H)

    ¿Qué hora es? What time is it? (H)

el **horno** oven (6)

hoy today (H)

    ¿Qué día es hoy? What day is today? (H)

el **huevo** egg (9)

    los huevos fritos fried eggs (9)

    los huevos pasados por agua hard-boiled eggs (9)

    los huevos revueltos scrambled eggs (9)

I

impaciente impatient (3)

el **impermeable** raincoat (2)

importante important (H)

el **inglés** English (H)

inteligente intelligent (3)

interesante interesting (H)

el **invierno** winter (H)

ir to go (H)

    ir a (+ *inf.*) to be going to (do something) (H)

    ¿Adónde vas? Where are you going? (4)

Voy a... I'm going to... (4)

irse (*reflexive*) to leave, to go away (11)

Me voy a la escuela.
I'm leaving for school. (Q)

J

el **jamón** (*pl.: jamones*) ham (9)

el **jardín** (*pl.: jardines*) garden (4)

joven (*pl.: jóvenes*) young (H)

el **jueves** Thursday (H)

los jueves on Thursdays (H)

jugar (u ➡ ue) to play (a game or sport) (H)

el **jugo** juice (9)

julio July (H)

junio June (H)

L

la (*f. s.*) the (H)

el **labio** lip (1)

lacio, lacia straight (hair) (3)

la **lámpara** lamp (5)

el **lápiz** (*pl.: lápices*) pencil (H)

largo, larga long (H)

las (*f. pl.*) the (H)

la **lata** can (6)

la **lavadora** washing machine (7)

el **lavaplatos** (*pl.: los lavaplatos*) dishwasher (6)

lavar to wash (7)

lavar la ropa to wash clothes, to do laundry (7)

lavarse (*reflexive*) to wash oneself (11)

le to him/her/you (*formal*) (H)

la **lección** (*pl.: lecciones*) lesson (H)

la **leche** milk (9)

la **lechuga** lettuce (10)

el **lector de DVD** DVD player (4)

la **lectura** reading (H)

leer to read (H)

lejos de far from (5)

la **lengua** tongue (1)

levantarse (*reflexive*) to get up, stand up (11)

el **libro** book (H)

la **licuadora** blender (6)

el **limón** (*pl.: limones*) lemon (8)

limpiar to clean (H), to wash (7)

limpiar el piso to clean/wash the floor (7)

limpio, limpia clean (7)

llamarse to be called (H)

¿Cómo te llamas?
What's your name? (H)

Me llamo... My name is... (H)

Se llama... His/Her name is... (H)

llevar to wear (2)

llover (o ➡ ue) to rain (H)

Llueve. It's raining. (H)

el **loro** parrot (H)

los (*m. pl.*) the (H)

luego (*adv.*) later, then (11)

¡Hasta luego! See you later! (H)

el **lunes** Monday (H)

los lunes on Mondays (H)

la **luz** (*pl.: luces*) light (H)

M

la **madrastra** stepmother (H)

la **madre** mother (H)

la **maestra** (female) teacher (H)

el **maestro** (male) teacher (H)

el **maíz** corn (10)

mal (*adj., before a m. s. noun*) bad; (*adv.*) not well, badly (H)

Hace mal tiempo.
The weather is bad. (H)

Me queda mal. It fits me badly. (2)

malo bad (H)

la **mamá** mother, mom (H)

la **mano** hand (1)

el **mantel** (*pl.: manteles*) tablecloth (8)

la **mantequilla** butter (9)

la **manzana** apple (8)

mañana *(adv.)* tomorrow (H)
  ¡Hasta mañana! See you
    tomorrow! (H)

la **mañana** morning (H)
  de/por la mañana in the morning
    (a. m.) (H)

el **mapa** map (H)

maravilloso, maravillosa
  wonderful (H)

el **marcador** marker (H)

la **margarina** margarine (9)

la **mariposa** butterfly (H)

marrón *(pl.: marrones)* brown (H)

el **martes** Tuesday (H)
  los martes on Tuesdays

marzo March (H)

más plus (H); more (3)
  el más, la más the most (12)
  más o menos so-so (H)
  más... que more... than (3)

las **matemáticas** mathematics (H)

mayo May (H)

la **mayonesa** mayonnaise (10)

me (to) me, myself (H)
  Me gusta... I like… (H)
  Me llamo... My name is… (H)

mediano, mediana medium (2)

la **medianoche** midnight (H)
  a medianoche at midnight (H)

las **medias** pantyhose, stockings (2)

medio, media half (H)
  media hora a half-hour (H)
  una hora y media an hour and a
    half (H)

el **mediodía** noon, midday (H)
  a mediodía at midday, noon (H)

la **mejilla** cheek (1)

menos to, of (time) (H); less,
  minus (3)
  menos... que less... than (3)

Son las dos menos cuarto. It's
  fifteen to two..., It's a quarter
  to (of) two. (H)

la **mermelada** jam, marmalade (9)

el **mes** *(pl.: meses)* month (H)

la **mesa** table (H)

la **mesita de noche** night table (5)

mi *(pl.: mis)* my (H)

el **microondas** microwave (oven) (6)

el **miedo** fear (H)
  tener miedo to be afraid,
    to be scared (H)

el **miércoles** Wednesday (H)
  los miércoles on Wednesdays (H)

el **minuto** minute (H)

mirar to look (at), to watch (6)

morado, morada purple (H)

la **mostaza** mustard (10)

mucho *(adv.)* a lot (H)
  mucho más a lot more (5)

mucho, mucha *(adj.)* much (9)

muchos, muchas *(adj.)* many (9)

los **muebles** furniture (5)

la **mujer** *(pl.: mujeres)* woman (H)

el **mundo** world (H)

la **música** music (H)

muy very (H)
  Muy bien, gracias. Very well,
    thank you. (H)

N

nada nothing (9)

nadar to swim (H)

la **naranja** orange (fruit) (8)

la **nariz** *(pl.: narices)* nose (1)

necesitar to need (6)

negro, negra black (H)

nevar (e ➡ ie) to snow (H)
  Nieva. It's snowing. (H)

la **nieta** granddaughter (H)

el **nieto** grandson (H)

los **nietos** grandsons, grandchildren (H)

la **niña** girl (H)

el **niño** boy (H)

no no, not (H)

la **noche** night, evening (H)

¡Buenas noches! Good evening!, Good night! (H)

nosotras *(f.)* we, us (4)

nosotros *(m.)* we, us (4)

noviembre November (H)

nublado, nublada cloudy (H)

Está nublado. It's cloudy. (H)

nuestro, nuestra, nuestros, nuestras our (9)

nuevo, nueva new (5)

el **número** number (H)

el número de teléfono telephone number (H)

nunca never (H)

O

octubre October (H)

la **oficina** office (12)

el **ojo** eye (1)

ondulado, ondulada wavy (hair) (3)

la **oreja** ear (1)

el **oso** bear (H)

el **otoño** fall, autumn (H)

P

el **padrastro** stepfather (H)

el **padre** father (H)

los **padres** parents, fathers (H)

el **pájaro** bird (H)

el **pan** bread (10)

el pan tostado toast (9)

los **pantalones** slacks, trousers, pants (2)

la **papa** potato (10)

el **papá** father, dad (H)

los **papás** parents, fathers (H)

el **papel** *(pl.: papeles)* paper (H)

la hoja de papel sheet of paper (H)

la **papelera** wastebasket (H)

la **pared** *(pl.: paredes)* wall (H)

el **parque** park (H)

la **parte** part (1)

participar to participate, to take part in (H)

pasar to pass (7)

pasar la aspiradora to vacuum (7)

el **pasillo** corridor, hall, hallway (4)

patinar to skate (H)

el **patio** courtyard, patio (4)

el **pavo** turkey (10)

peinarse *(reflexive)* to comb one's hair (11)

pelirrojo redheaded (3)

el **pelo** hair (1)

el pelo canoso gray hair (3)

el pelo castaño brown hair (3)

el pelo lacio straight hair (3)

el pelo ondulado wavy hair (3)

el pelo rizado curly hair (3)

el pelo rojizo red hair (3)

el pelo rubio blond hair (3)

pensar (e ➡ ie) *(+ inf.)* to think (of doing), to plan (to do) (11)

pequeño, pequeña small, little (H)

la **pera** pear (8)

pero but (4)

el **perro** dog (H)

la **persona** person (3)

el **pescado** (in cooking) fish (10)

las **pestañas** eyelashes (1)

el **pez** *(pl.: peces)* (live) fish (H)

el **pie** *(pl.: pies)* foot (1)

la **pierna** leg (1)

el **pijama** pajamas (2)

la **pimienta** pepper (8)

pintar to paint (H)

la **piña** pineapple (8)

el **piso** floor (5)

el **pizarrón** chalkboard, blackboard, whiteboard (H)

la **plancha** iron (appliance) (7)

planchar to iron (7)

planchar la ropa to iron clothes (7)

la **planta** plant (7)

regar las plantas to water the plants (7)

el **plátano** banana (8)

el **platillo** saucer (8)

el **plato** dish, plate (8)

pobre poor

poco little (amount) (9)

pocos, pocas few (9)

poder (o ➜ ue) to be able (9)

el **pollo** chicken (10)

el **polvo** dust (7)

quitar el polvo to dust (7)

poner to set, to place (8)

poner la mesa to set the table (8)

ponerse *(reflexive)* to put on, to wear (11)

ponerse la ropa to get dressed (11)

popular popular (3)

por in (time) (H)

por la mañana in the morning (H)

por la tarde in the afternoon (H)

por la noche in the evening (H)

¡Por favor! Please! (9)

¿Por qué? Why? (H)

¿Por qué no? Why not? (H)

¡Por supuesto! Of course! (1)

por último finally, last (11)

practicar to practice (H)

practicar deportes to practice (play) sports (H)

la **prima** (female) cousin (H)

la **primavera** spring (H)

primero, primera *(adj.)* first (H)

el **primero** the first (of the month) (H)

el **primo** (male) cousin (H)

los **primos** cousins (H)

la **prisa** hurry (H)

tener prisa to be in a hurry (H)

probar (o ➜ ue) to taste, to try (10)

pronto soon (H)

¡Hasta pronto! See you soon! (H)

próximo, próxima next (H)

la próxima semana next week (H)

la **puerta** door (H)

la **puesta del sol** sunset (H)

el **pupitre** student's desk (H)

Q

que than (3)

más... que more... than (3)

menos... que less... than (3)

¿Qué? What? (H)

¿Qué tal? How's it going? (H)

¿Qué tienes? What's the matter? What do you have? (H)

¿Qué vas a comprar? What are you going to buy? (2)

quedar to fit (clothes) (2)

Me queda bien/mal. It fits me well/badly. (2)

el **quehacer** *(pl.: quehaceres)* chore (7)

querer (e ➜ ie) to want (9)

el **queso** cheese (9)

¿Quién? Who? (H)

¿Quién es...? Who is...? (H)

quitar to remove, to take off (7)

quitarse la ropa to undress, to take off one's clothes (11)

R

el **radio** radio (5)

el **ratón** *(pl.: ratones)* mouse (H)

la **razón** *(pl.: razones)* reason (H)

tener razón to be right (H)

recoger to pick up, to clean up (7)

recoger las cosas to straighten up (7)

el **rectángulo** rectangle (H)

el **refrigerador** *(pl.: refrigeradores)* refrigerator (6)

regar **(i ➡ ie) las plantas** to water
  the plants (7)
la **regla** ruler (H)
el **reloj** (*pl.: relojes*) clock (H)
el **retrato** portrait (5)
  rizado, rizada curly (hair) (3)
la **rodilla** knee (1)
  rojizo, rojiza red (hair) (3)
  rojo, roja red (H)
la **ropa** clothes, clothing (2)
el **ropero** closet, wardrobe (5)
  rosado, rosada pink (H)
  rubio, rubia blond (hair) (3)

S

el **sábado** Saturday (H)
  los sábados on Saturdays (H)
  saber (*+ inf.*) to know how to
    (do something) (12)
  ¿Sabías que...?
    Did you know that...? (H)
  sacar to take out, to get out (7)
    sacar la basura to take out
      the trash (7)
la **sal** salt (8)
la **sala de estar** living room (4)
la **salida** exit (12)
la **salida del sol** sunrise (H)
el **salón de clase** classroom (H)
la **salsa de tomate** tomato sauce,
    ketchup (10)
la **salud** health (H)
la **sandía** watermelon (8)
el **sándwich** (*pl.: sándwiches*)
    sandwich (10)
la **secadora** dryer (7)
  secar to dry (7)
    secar la ropa to dry clothes (7)
  secarse (*reflexive*) to dry oneself (11)
la **sed** thirst (H)
    tener sed to be thirsty (H)
la **semana** week (H)

  el día de la semana weekday (H)
  el fin de semana weekend (H)
  esta semana this week (H)
  la próxima semana next week (H)
  sensacional sensational (H)
  señor, Sr. Mr. (H)
el **señor** man, gentleman (H)
  señora, Sra. Mrs., ma'am (H)
la **señora** woman, lady (H)
  señorita, Srta. Miss (H)
la **señorita** young lady (H)
  septiembre September (H)
  ser to be (H)
    eres you (*familiar*) are (3)
    es he/she is, you (*formal*) are (3)
    son they are (3)
    soy I am (H, 3)
la **servilleta** napkin (8)
  sí yes (H)
  siempre always (H)
la **silla** chair (H)
el **sillón** (*pl.: sillones*) armchair (5)
  simpático, simpática nice,
    pleasant (H)
  sin without (7)
  sobre on, on top of, over (8)
el **sofá** sofa (5)
el **sol** sun (H)
    Hace sol. It's sunny. (H)
    la puesta del sol sunset (H)
    la salida del sol sunrise (H)
el **sombrero** hat (2)
la **sopa** soup (10)
el **sótano** basement, cellar (4)
  Sr. (see *señor*)
  Sra. (see *señora*)
  Srta. (see *señorita*)
  su (*pl.: sus*) his, her, your (*formal*),
    their (H)
  subir to go up (12)
    subir las escaleras to go up
      the stairs (12)

sucio, sucia   dirty (7)

el **sueño**   sleep (H)

   tener sueño   to be sleepy (H)

la **suerte**   luck (H)

   tener suerte   to be lucky (H)

el **suéter**   (*pl.: suéteres*)   sweater (2)

T

también   also, too (H)

tampoco   neither, either (H)

la **tarde**   afternoon, evening (H)

   ¡Buenas tardes!   Good afternoon!,
     Good evening! (H)

   de/por la tarde   in the afternoon
     (p. m.) (H)

la **taza**   cup (8)

te   to you (*familiar*), yourself (H)

   te duele (n)...   your... hurt(s) (1)

   te queda (n)...   (it) fit(s) you,
     look(s)...on you (2)

el **té**   tea (9)

el **techo**   ceiling (4)

el **teléfono**   telephone (H)

la **televisión**   television (program) (6)

el **televisor**   television set (5)

el **tenedor**   fork (8)

tener   to have (H)

   ¿Qué tienes?   What's the matter?
     What do you have? (H)

   tener que (+ *inf.*)   to have to
     (do something) (7)

terrible   terrible (H)

la **tía**   aunt (H)

el **tiempo**   weather, time (H)

   Hace buen tiempo.   The weather is
     nice. (H)

   Hace mal tiempo.   The weather is
     bad. (H)

   ¿Qué tiempo hace?   What's the
     weather like? (H)

la **tienda**   store (H)

el **tigre**   tiger (H)

tímido, tímida   shy (3)

el **tío**   uncle (H)

los **tíos**   aunts and uncles, uncles (H)

la **tiza**   chalk (H)

el **tobillo**   ankle (1)

el **tocador**   (*pl.: tocadores*)   dresser (5)

tocar   to touch (1)

el **tocino**   bacon (9)

todos, todas   all, every (5)

tomar   to have (meals), to drink (9)

   tomar el desayuno
     to have breakfast (9)

el **tomate**   tomato (10)

   la salsa de tomate   tomato sauce,
     ketchup (10)

la **toronja**   grapefruit (9)

tostado, tostada   toasted (9)

   el pan tostado   toast (bread) (9)

el **tostador**   toaster (6)

trabajar   to work (H)

traer   to bring (8)

el **traje de baño**   swimsuit (2)

el **trapeador**   mop (7)

el **trapo**   rag (7)

el **triángulo**   triangle (H)

tu (*pl.: tus*)   your (*familiar*) (H)

tú   you (*familiar*) (H)

U

último, última   last (11)

   por último   lastly (11)

un, una   a, an (H)

unas (*f. pl.*)   some, a few (H)

la **unidad** (*pl.: unidades*)   unit (H)

unos (*m. pl.*)   some, a few (H)

¡Úsalo!   Use it! (H)

usar   to use (H)

   usar la computadora   to use the
     computer (H)

usted (*s. formal; pl.: ustedes*)   you (H)

la **uva**   grape (8)

V

el **vaso** glass (8)

veces, a sometimes (H)

la **ventana** window (H)

el **ventilador** fan (5)

el **verano** summer (H)

¿Verdad? Right? (5)

verde green (H)

la **verdura** vegetable (10)

el **vestido** dress (2)

vez time; occasion (H)

a **veces** sometimes (H)

la **videocasetera** VCR (5)

viejo, vieja old (H)

el **viento** wind (H)

Hace viento. It's windy. (H)

el **viernes** Friday (H)

los viernes on Fridays (H)

vivir to live (6)

volver (o ➡ ue) to return (11)

Y

y and (H)

¿Y tú? And you? (H)

yo I (H)

Z

la **zanahoria** carrot (10)

el **zapato** shoe (2)

Word List

English-Spanish

This list gives the English translation of Spanish words that you've learned in *¿Qué tal?* A number in parentheses indicates the unit where a word is taught. (H) indicates that a word was first presented in *¡Hola!*

A

a, an   un *(m.)*, una *(f.)* (H)
a lot   mucho (H)
administrative assistant   el asistente administrativo, la asistente administrativa (12)
afternoon   la tarde (H)
all   todos, todas (5)
also   también (H)
always   siempre (H)
among   entre (H)
amusing   divertido, divertida (H)
and   y (H)
animal   el animal *(pl.:* animales) (H)
ankle   el tobillo (1)
apartment   el apartamento (4)
apple   la manzana (8)
April   abril (H)
arm   el brazo (1)
armchair   el sillón (5)
art   el arte (H)
at   a (H)
athletic   atlético, atlética (3)
attic   el ático (4)
auditorium   el auditorio (12)

August   agosto (H)
aunt   la tía (H)
aunts and uncles   los tíos (H)
autumn   el otoño (H)

B

back   la espalda (1)
   in back of   detrás de (5)
bacon   el tocino (9)
bad   mal *(adj.; before a m. s. noun)*, malo, mala (H)
badly   mal (H)
balcony   el balcón (4)
ballpoint pen   el bolígrafo (H)
banana   el plátano (8)
basement   el sótano (4)
bath, to take a   bañarse (11)
bathing suit   el traje de baño (2)
bathrobe   la bata (2)
bathroom   el cuarto de baño (4)
to **be**   (in a place, for a time) estar; (a quality or permanent state) ser (H)
   to **be able to**   poder (o ➡ ue) (9)
   to **be called**   llamarse (H)
   to **be cold**   tener frío (e ➡ ie) (H)
   to **be going to**   ir a *(+ inf.)* (H)

to **be hot**   tener calor (e ➡ ie) (H)

to **be scared**   tener miedo
(e ➡ ie) (H)

to **be sleepy**   tener sueño
(e ➡ ie) (H)

beans   los frijoles (10)

bear   el oso (H)

to **beat**   batir (food) (6)

bed   la cama (5)

bedroom   el dormitorio (4)

before   antes (7)

to **begin**   comenzar (e ➡ ie) (11)

behind   detrás de (5)

beneath   debajo de (8)

big   grande (H)

bird   el pájaro (H)

birthday   el cumpleaños (H)

When is your birthday?
¿Cuándo es tu cumpleaños? (H)

Happy birthday!
¡Feliz cumpleanos! (H)

black   negro, negra (H)

blackboard   el pizarrón (H)

blender   la licuadora (6)

blond   rubio, rubia (3)

blouse   la blusa (2)

blue   azul (H)

body   el cuerpo (1)

book   el libro (H)

bookcase   la estantería (5)

boots   las botas (2)

boring   aburrido, aburrida (H)

bowl   el bol (*pl.:* boles) (6)

box   la caja (6)

boy   el chico, el niño (H)

bread   el pan (10)

breakfast   el desayuno (9)

to **bring**   traer (8)

broom   la escoba (7)

brother   el hermano (H)

brothers and sisters
los hermanos (H)

brown   marrón (H)

brown   (hair, eyes) castaño (3)

to **brush**   cepillar (11)

to **brush one's teeth**   cepillarse los
dientes (11)

but   pero (3)

butter   la mantequilla (9)

butterfly   la mariposa (H)

to **buy**   comprar (H)

C

cabinet   el gabinete (6)

cafeteria   la cafetería (12)

calendar   el calendario (H)

can *(noun)*   la lata (6)

can opener   el abrelatas (6)

canary   el canario (H)

cap   la gorra (2)

carpet   la alfombra (5)

carrot   la zanahoria (10)

cat   el gato (H)

ceiling   el techo (4)

to **celebrate**   celebrar (H)

cereal   el cereal (9)

chair   la silla (H)

chalk   la tiza (H)

chalkboard   el pizarrón (H)

chalk eraser   el borrador (H)

cheek   la mejilla (1)

cheese   el queso (9)

cherry   la cereza (8)

chicken   el pollo (10)

children   los hijos, los niños (H)

chimney   la chimenea (4)

chocolate   el chocolate (9)

chore   el quehacer (*pl.* quehaceres) (7)

circle   el círculo (H)

class   la clase (H)

classroom   el salón de clase (H)

clean   limpio, limpia (7)

to **clean** limpiar (7)

to **clean/wash the floor** limpiar el
piso (7)

clock el reloj (H)

to **close** cerrar (e ➡ ie) (11)

closet el ropero (5)

clothes la ropa (2)

cloudy nublado, nublada (H)

It's cloudy. Está nublado. (H)

coat el abrigo (2)

coffee el café (9)

cold frío (H)

I'm cold. Tengo frío. (H)

It's cold. Hace frío. (H)

color el color (H)

to **comb one's hair** peinarse (*reflexive*)
(11)

computer la computadora (H)

connection conexión (H)

cook el cocinero, la cocinera (12)

to **cook** cocinar (6)

cool fresco, fresca (H)

It's cool. (weather) Hace fresco. (H)

corn el maíz (10)

corridor el pasillo (4)

courtyard el patio (4)

cousin el primo, la prima (H)

cousins los primos (H)

cream la crema (8)

cup la taza (8)

curly (hair) rizado, rizada (3)

curtains las cortinas (5)

custodian el conserje, la conserje (12)

D

dad el papá (H)

to **dance** bailar (H)

date la fecha (H)

What's today's date? ¿Qué fecha
es hoy? (H)

daughter la hija (H)

day el día (H)

December diciembre (H)

to **descend** bajar (12)

desk (student's) el pupitre (H);
(large) el escritorio (H)

difficult difícil (*pl.*: difíciles) (H)

dining room el comedor (4)

dinner la cena (10)

director el director, la directora (12)

dirty sucio, sucia (7)

dish el plato (8)

dishwasher el lavaplatos
(*pl.*: los lavaplatos) (6)

to **do** hacer (6)

to do the laundry lavar la ropa (7)

dog el perro (H)

door la puerta (H)

down the stairs, to go bajar las
escaleras (12)

to **draw** dibujar (H)

drawer el cajón (*pl.*: *cajones*) (6)

dress el vestido (2)

dresser el tocador (5)

to **drink** beber (9)

drinking fountain la fuente de
agua (12)

to **dry** secar (7)

to dry the clothes secar la ropa (7)

to **dry oneself** secarse (*reflexive*) (11)

dryer la secadora (7)

dust el polvo (7)

to **dust** quitar el polvo (7)

DVD el DVD (disc) (5)

DVD player el lector de DVD (5)

E

ear la oreja (1)

easy fácil (*pl.*: *fáciles*) (H)

to **eat** comer (6)

to eat breakfast tomar el
desayuno (9)

to eat lunch almorzar
(o ➡ ue) (10)

egg el huevo (9)
  fried eggs los huevos fritos (9)
  hard-boiled eggs los huevos
    pasados por agua (9)
  scrambled eggs los huevos
    revueltos (9)
either tampoco (H)
elbow el codo (1)
electric mixer
  la batidora eléctrica (6)
electrical socket el enchufe (6)
end el fin (*pl.*: fines) (H)
English el inglés (H)
entertaining divertido, divertida (H)
entrance la entrada (12)
equator el ecuador (H)
eraser el borrador (H)
evening la tarde, la noche (H)
exit la salida (12)
eye el ojo (1)
eyebrow la ceja (1)
eyelashes las pestañas (1)

F

face la cara (1)
fall el otoño (H)
family la familia (H)
fan el ventilador (5)
fantastic fantástico, fantástica (H)
far from lejos de (5)
fat gordo, gorda (H)
father el padre (H)
faucet el grifo (6)
favor el favor (9)
favorite favorito, favorita (H)
fear el miedo (H)
February febrero (H)
fence la cerca (4)
few pocos, pocas (9)
few, a unos, unas (H)
fine bien (H)
finger el dedo (1)

to **finish** acabar (7)
first, the el primero (H)
fish (in cooking) el pescado (10)
fish (live) el pez (*pl.:* peces) (H)
to **fit** (clothes) quedar (2)
flag la bandera (H)
flamingo el flamenco (H)
floor el piso (5)
flu la gripe (H)
foot el pie (1)
forehead la frente (1)
fork el tenedor (8)
fountain la fuente (12)
Friday el viernes (H)
  on Fridays los viernes (H)
fried frito, frita (9)
friendly simpático, simpática (H)
friends amigos (H)
from de (H)
fruit la fruta (8)
fun divertido, divertida (H)
funny cómico, cómica (3)
furniture los muebles (5)

G

garage el garaje (4)
garden el jardín (*pl.:* jardines) (4)
generous generoso, generosa (3)
gentleman el señor (H)
to **get dressed** ponerse la ropa
    (*reflexive*) (11)
to **get up** levantarse (*reflexive*) (11)
girl la chica, la niña (H)
glass el vaso (8)
globe el globo (H)
to **go** ir (H)
  to go away irse (*reflexive*) (11)
  to go to bed acostarse (*reflexive*)
    (o ➡ ue) (11)
  to go down the stairs bajar (12)
  to go up the stairs subir (12)

good   buen (*before a s. m. noun*), bueno, buena (H)

good-looking   guapo, guapa (H)

Good afternoon.   Buenas tardes. (H)

Good-bye!   ¡Adiós! (H)

Good evening.   Buenas noches. (H)

Good morning.   Buenos días. (H)

Good night.   Buenas noches. (H)

grandchildren   los nietos (H)

granddaughter   la nieta (H)

grandfather   el abuelo (H)

grandmother   la abuela (H)

grandparents   los abuelos (H)

grandson   el nieto (H)

grape   la uva (8)

grapefruit   la toronja (9)

gray   gris (H); canoso (hair) (3)

great-grandfather   el bisabuelo (H)

great-grandmother   la bisabuela (H)

great-grandparents
   los bisabuelos (H)

green   verde (H)

gymnasium   el gimnasio (H)

H

hair   el pelo (1)

half   medio, media (H)
   half-hour, a   media hora (H)

hallway   el pasillo (4)

ham   el jamón (9)

hamburger   la hamburguesa (10)

hand   la mano (1)

to **hang up**   colgar (o ➡ ue) (7)
   to hang up clothes
      colgar la ropa (Q)

happy   feliz (*pl.:* felices) (H)
   Happy birthday!
      ¡Feliz cumpleaños! (H)

hat   el sombrero (2)

to **have**   tener (H); tomar (meals) (9)
   to have breakfast
      tomar el desayuno (9)

to have just   acabar de + *inf.* (7)

to have to   tener que + *inf.* (7)

he   él (H)

head   la cabeza (1)

health   la salud (H)

heat   el calor (H)

Hello!   ¡Hola! (H)

her   su (*pl.: sus*) (H)

Hi!   ¡Hola! (H)

his   su (*pl.: sus*) (H)

home   la casa (H)

hot   calor
   It's hot.   Hace calor. (H)
   I'm hot.   Tengo calor. (H)

hour   la hora (H)
   hour and a half, an
      una hora y media (H)
   hour and a quarter, an
      una hora y cuarto (H)

house   la casa (H)

How?   ¿Cómo? (H)
   How are you?   ¿Cómo estás?
      (*familiar*) (H)
   **How are you doing? How's it
      going?**   ¿Qué tal? (H)
   How do you say it?   ¿Cómo se
      dice? (H)
   How many...?   ¿Cuántos...?,
      ¿Cuántas...? (H)
   How much...?   ¿Cuánto...?,
      ¿Cuánta...? (H)

hunger   el hambre (*f.*) (H)

hungry, to be   tener hambre (H)

hurry   la prisa (H)
   hurry, to be in a   tener prisa (H)

to **hurt**   doler (o ➡ ue) (1)
   My head hurts.   Me duele la
      cabeza. (1)

I

I   yo (H)

ice cream   el helado (H)

impatient impaciente (3)
important importante (H)
in en (H)
in back of detrás de (5)
in front of delante de (5)
infirmary la enfermería (12)
inside dentro de (4)
intelligent inteligente (3)
interesting interesante (H)
iron (appliance) la plancha (7)
to **iron** planchar (7)
It's... Es... (H)
  It's cloudy. Está nublado. (H)
  It's cold. Hace frío. (H)
  It's cool. Hace fresco. (H)
  It's hot. Hace calor. (H)
  It's raining. Llueve. (H)
  It's snowing. Nieva. (H)
  It's sunny. Hace sol. (H)
  It's windy. Hace viento. (H)

J

jacket la chaqueta (2)
jam la mermelada (9)
janitor el conserje, la conserje (12)
January enero (H)
juice el jugo (9)
July julio (H)
June junio (H)

K

ketchup la salsa de tomate (10)
kitchen la cocina (4)
knee la rodilla (1)
knife el cuchillo (8)
to **know how to** (do something)
  saber (+ *inf.*) (12)
  Did you know that...?
    ¿Sabías que...? (H)

L

lady la señora (H)
  young lady la señorita (H)
lamp la lámpara (5)
large grande (H)
last último, última (11)
last (*adv.*) por último (11)
to **learn** aprender (H)
to **leave** irse (*reflexive*) (11)
leg la pierna (1)
lemon el limón (*pl.*: limones) (8)
less menos (3)
  less... than menos... que (3)
lesson la lección (*pl.*: lecciones) (H)
lettuce la lechuga (10)
librarian el bibliotecario,
  la bibliotecaria (12)
library la biblioteca (H)
to **lie down** acostarse
  (*reflexive*) (o ➡ ue) (11)
light la luz (*pl.*: luces) (H)
light bulb la bombilla (6)
to **like** gustar (H)
  What do you like to do? ¿Qué te
    gusta hacer? (H)
lip el labio (1)
to **listen** escuchar (H)
little pequeño, pequeña (H);
  (amount) poco (9)
to **live** vivir (6)
living room la sala de estar (4)
long largo, larga (H)
to **look (at)** mirar (6)
luck la suerte (H)
lucky, to be tener suerte (H)
lunch el almuerzo (10)

M

mailbox el buzón (*pl.*: buzones) (4)
to **make** hacer (H)
man el hombre (H)

many   muchos, muchas (9)
map   el mapa (H)
March   marzo (H)
margarine   la margarina (9)
marker   el marcador (H)
marmalade   la mermelada (9)
marvelous   maravilloso,
   maravillosa (H)
mathematics   las matemáticas (H)
May   mayo (H)
mayonnaise   la mayonesa (10)
meat   la carne (10)
meatballs   las albóndigas (10)
medium   mediano, mediana (2)
microwave   (oven) el microondas (6)
midday   el mediodía (H)
   at midday   a mediodía (H)
midnight   la medianoche (H)
   at midnight   a medianoche (H)
milk   la leche (9)
minute   el minuto (H)
mirror   el espejo (5)
Miss   Señorita (Srta.) (H)
mom   la mamá (H)
Monday   el lunes (H)
   on Mondays   los lunes (H)
month   el mes (*pl.: meses*) (H)
mop   el trapeador (7)
more   más (H)
   a lot more   mucho más (5)
more... than   más... que (3)
morning   la mañana (H)
   in the morning
      de/por la mañana (H)
most, the   el más, la más (12)
mother   la madre (H)
mouse   el ratón (*pl.: ratones*) (H)
mouth   la boca (1)
movie theater   el cine (H)
Mr.   Señor (Sr.) (H)
Mrs.   Señora (Sra.) (H)
much   mucho, mucha (9)

music   la música (H)
mustard   la mostaza (10)
my   mi (*pl.:* mis) (H)

N

name   el nombre (H)
   My name is...   Me llamo... (H)
napkin   la servilleta (8)
near   cerca de (5)
neck   el cuello (1)
to **need**   necesitar (6)
neither   tampoco (H)
never   nunca (H)
new   nuevo, nueva (5)
next   próximo, próxima (H)
   next week   la próxima semana (H)
nice   simpático, simpática (H)
night   la noche (H)
   Good evening! Good night!
      ¡Buenas noches! (H)
night table   la mesita de noche (5)
no   no (H)
noodles   los espaguetis (10)
noon   el mediodía (H)
   at noon   a mediodía (H)
nose   la nariz, (*pl.:* narices) (1)
not   no (H)
notebook   el cuaderno (H)
nothing   nada (9)
November   noviembre (H)
now   ahora (H)
number   el número (H)
nurse   el enfermero, la enfermera (12)
   nurse's office   là enfermería (12)

O

oatmeal   la avena (9)
October   octubre (H)
of   de (H)
   ¡Of course!   ¡Claro!, ¡Claro que sí!
      (H); ¡Por supuesto! (1)

office el despacho, la oficina (12)
Oh! ¡Ay! (H)
old viejo, vieja (H)
on en (8)
  on top of en (8)
to **open** abrir (6)
orange (color) anaranjado, anaranjada (H)
orange (fruit) la naranja (8)
our nuestro, nuestra *(s.);* nuestros, nuestras *(pl.)* (9)
outside *(adv.)* fuera de (4)
oven el horno (6)

P

to **paint** pintar (H)
painting el cuadro (5)
pajamas el pijama (2)
pants los pantalones (2)
pantyhose las medias (2)
paper el papel *(pl.:* papeles) (H)
parents los papás, los padres (H)
park el parque (H)
parrot el loro (H)
part la parte (1)
to **participate** participar (H)
patio el patio (4)
pea el guisante (10)
peach el durazno (8)
peanut butter la crema de cacahuate (10)
pear la pera (8)
pen (ballpoint) el bolígrafo (H)
pencil el lápiz *(pl.:* lápices) (H)
pepper la pimienta (8)
person la persona (3)
physical education la educación física (H)
to **pick up** recoger (7)
pillow la almohada (5)
pineapple la piña (8)
pink rosado, rosada (H)

to **plan** (to do something)
    pensar + *inf.* (e ➡ ie) (11)
plant la planta (7)
plate el plato (8)
to **play** jugar (u ➡ ue) (H)
to **play sports** practicar deportes
    (u ➡ ue) (H)
pleasant simpático, simpática (3)
please por favor (9)
to **please** gustar (H)
plug el enchufe (6)
plus más (H)
poor pobre
popular popular (3)
portrait el retrato (5)
poster el cartel (5)
potato la papa (10)
to **practice** practicar (H)
pretty bonito, bonita (2)
principal el director, la directora (12)
purple morado, morada (H)
to **put** poner (8)
    to put on ponerse *(reflexive)* (11)

Q

quarter el cuarto (H)
  quarter-hour, a
    un cuarto de hora (H)
  an hour and a quarter
    una hora y cuarto (H)

R

rabbit el conejo (H)
radio el radio (5)
rag el trapo (7)
to **rain** llover (o ➡ ue) (H)
    It's raining. Llueve. (H)
raincoat el impermeable (2)
to **read** leer (H)
reading *(noun)* la lectura (H)
reason la razón (H)
rectangle el rectángulo (H)

red rojo, roja (H)

  red (hair) rojizo, rojiza (3)

  redheaded pelirrojo (3)

refrigerator el refrigerador
(*pl.:* refrigeradores) (6)

to **return** volver (o ➡ ue) (11)

rice el arroz (10)

right, to be tener razón (H)

robe la bata (2)

room el cuarto (4)

rug la alfombra (5)

ruler la regla (H)

to **run** correr (6)

S

salad la ensalada (10)

salt la sal (8)

sandwich el sándwich
(*pl.:* sándwiches) (10)

Saturday el sábado (H)

  on Saturdays los sábados

saucer el platillo (8)

school la escuela (H)

school principal el director,
la directora (12)

science las ciencias (H)

season la estación (*pl.:* estaciones) (H)

See you later. Hasta luego. (H)

See you soon. Hasta pronto. (H)

See you tomorrow. Hasta
mañana. (H)

sensational sensacional (H)

September septiembre (H)

to **set the table** poner la mesa (8)

she ella (H)

sheet of paper la hoja de papel (H)

shelf el estante (5)

shirt la camisa (2)

shoe el zapato (2)

short (length) corto, corta;
(height) bajo, baja (H)

shoulder el hombro (1)

to **shower, take a** ducharse *(reflexive)* (11)

to **shut** cerrar (e ➡ ie) (11)

shy tímido, tímida (3)

to **sing** cantar (H)

sink el fregadero (6)

sister la hermana (H)

to **skate** patinar (H)

skirt la falda (2)

slacks los pantalones (2)

sleep sueño (H)

sleepy, to be tener sueño (H)

small pequeño, paqueña (H)

to **snow** nevar (e ➡ ie) (H)

  It's snowing. Nieva. (H)

so así (H)

social studies los estudios
sociales (H)

sock el calcetín (*pl.: calcetines*) (2)

sofa el sofá (5)

some unos, unas (H)

sometimes a veces (H)

son el hijo (H)

  sons, sons and daughters
los hijos (H)

soon pronto (H)

  See you soon! ¡Hasta pronto! (H)

so-so así, así; más o menos (H)

sound system el estéreo (5)

soup la sopa (10)

soupspoon la cuchara (8)

spaghetti los espaguetis (10)

  spaghetti with meatballs
los espaguetis con albóndigas (10)

Spanish el español (H)

to **speak** hablar (H)

spoon la cuchara (8)

sports los deportes (H)

  to play sports
practicar deportes (H)

spring la primavera (H)

square el cuadrado (H)

stairs las escaleras (4)

to **start** comenzar (e ➡ ie) (11)
stepbrother el hermanastro (H)
stepfather el padrastro (H)
stepmother la madrastra (H)
stepsister la hermanastra (H)
stereo el estéreo (5)
stockings las medias (2)
store la tienda (H)
stove la estufa (6)
straight (hair) lacio (3)
strawberry la fresa (8)
strong fuerte (3)
student el alumno, la alumna (H)
study (room) el despacho (4)
to **study** estudiar (H)
sugar el azúcar (8)
summer el verano (H)
sun el sol (H)
Sunday el domingo (H)
  on Sundays los domingos
sunrise la salida del sol (H)
sunset la puesta del sol (H)
supper la cena (10)
sweater el suéter (2)
to **sweep** barrer (7)
to **swim** nadar (H)
swimsuit el traje de baño (2)

T

table la mesa (H)
tablecloth el mantel
  (*pl.*: manteles) (8)
tablespoon la cuchara (8)
to **take** tomar (9)
  to take a shower ducharse (11)
  to take off one's clothes quitarse
    la ropa (11)
  to take out the trash sacar la
    basura (7)
  to take part in participar (H)
to **talk** hablar (H)
tall alto, alta (H)

to **taste** probar (o ➡ ue) (10)
tea el té (9)
teacher el maestro, la maestra (H)
teaspoon la cucharita (8)
telephone el teléfono (H)
telephone number el número de
  teléfono (H)
television (program) la televisión (6)
television set el televisor (5)
terrible terrible (H)
thank you gracias (H)
thanks gracias (H)
the (*s. m. f.*) el, la; (*pl.*) los, las (H)
their su, sus (H)
then luego (11)
there is, there are hay (H)
thin flaco, flaca (H)
think pensar (e ➡ ie) (11)
  to think of doing pensar
    (+ *inf.*) (11)
thirst la sed (H)
thirsty, to be tener sed (H)
this week esta semana (H)
Thursday el jueves (H)
  on Thursdays los jueves (H)
tiger el tigre (H)
time el tiempo; la hora (H)
timid tímido, tímida (3)
to a (H)
toast el pan tostado (9)
toasted tostado, tostada (9)
toaster el tostador (6)
today hoy (H)
tomato el tomate (10)
  tomato sauce la salsa
    de tomate (10)
tomorrow mañana (H)
  See you tomorrow! ¡Hasta
    mañana! (H)
tongue la lengua (1)
too también (H)
tooth el diente (1)

to **touch** tocar (1)

trash la basura (7)

triangle el triángulo (H)

to **try** probar (o ➡ ue) (10)

T-shirt la camiseta (2)

Tuesday el martes (H)

on Tuesdays los martes (H)

turkey el pavo (10)

U

ugly feo, fea (2)

uncle el tío (H)

uncles, uncles and aunts
los tíos (H)

under(neath) debajo de (8)

undershirt la camiseta (2)

to **understand** comprender (H)

to **undress** quitarse la ropa
(*reflexive*) (11)

unit la unidad (*pl.:* unidades) (H)

unpleasant antipático, antipática (H)

until hasta (H)

to **use** usar (H)

to **use the computer**
usar la computadora (H)

V

to **vacuum** pasar la aspiradora (7)

vacuum cleaner la aspiradora (7)

VCR la videocasetera (5)

vegetable la verdura (10)

very muy (H)

very well muy bien (H)

W

waist la cintura (1)

to **wake up** despertarse (*reflexive*)
(e ➡ ie) (11)

to **walk** caminar (H)

wall la pared (H)

to **want** querer (e ➡ ie) (9)

to **wash** lavar (7)

to wash clothes
lavar la ropa (7)

to wash oneself
lavarse (*reflexive*) (11)

to wash the floor
limpiar el piso (7)

washing machine la lavadora (7)

wastebasket la papelera (H)

water el agua (*f.*) (9)

water fountain la fuente
de agua (12)

watermelon la sandía (8)

to **water the plants** regar las plantas
(e ➡ ie) (7)

wavy (hair) ondulado (3)

we nosotros, nosotras (4)

weak débil (3)

to **wear** llevar (2); ponerse
(*reflexive*) (11)

weather el tiempo (H)

Wednesday el miércoles (H)

on Wednesdays los miércoles (H)

week la semana (H)

weekday el día de la semana (H)

weekend el fin de semana (H)

Welcome! ¡Bienvenidos! (H)

well bien (H)

It fits me well. Me queda bien. (2)

What? ¿Qué?, ¿Cómo? (H)

At what time? ¿A qué hora? (H)

What are you going to do? ¿Qué
vas a hacer? (H)

What color is it? ¿De qué color
es? (H)

What do you have? ¿Qué
tienes? (H)

What is it? ¿Qué es? (H)

What's (the boy's) name? ¿Cómo
se llama (el chico)? (H)

What's the weather like? ¿Qué
tiempo hace? (H)

What's your name? ¿Cómo te llamas? (H)

What's your phone number? ¿Cuál es tu número de teléfono? (H)

When? ¿Cuándo? (H)

Where? ¿Dónde?, ¿Adónde? (H)

Which? *(s.)* ¿Cuál?, *(pl.)* ¿Cuáles? (H)

Which season do you like? ¿Cuál estación te gusta? (H)

to **whip** (food) batir (6)

white blanco, blanca (H)

Who? *(s.)* ¿Quién? *(pl.)* ¿Quiénes? (H)

Who is...? ¿Quién es...? (H)

Whose? ¿De quién? (H)

Why? ¿Por qué? (H)

Why not? ¿Por qué no? (H)

window la ventana (H)

winter el invierno (H)

with con (7)

without sin (7)

woman la mujer (H)

wonderful maravilloso, maravillosa (H)

to **work** trabajar (12)

to **write** escribir (H)

y

years old, to be... tener... años (H)

yellow amarillo, amarilla (H)

yes sí (H)

you *(familiar)* tú; *(formal)* usted *(pl.: ustedes)* (H)

young joven *(pl.: jóvenes)* (H)

young woman/lady la señorita (H)

your *(familiar)* tu *(pl.: tus)*; *(formal)* su *(pl.: sus)* (H)

Index

Acknowledgments

Cover (t)Jamie Trapp, (c)Globe Turner, LLC/GeoNova Maps/Getty Images, (bl)Linda More/iStock/Getty Images, (bc) Brand X Pictures/Stockbyte/Getty Images, (br)Frans Lemmens/The Image Bank/Getty Images; 2-3 ©Peter Horree/Alamy; 3 (t)©Robert Landau/Alamy, (cr)©Kike Calvo/VWPICS/Alamy; 4 ©Lee Foster/Alamy; 16 ©Pablo Corral V/Corbis; 20 Todd Warnock/Photodisc/Getty Images; 22-23 ©Kevin Schafer/Corbis; 23 (t)©Rachael Bowes/Alamy, (b)©Gary Conner/Photo Edit Inc.; 30 ©Ricahrd A. Cooke/Corbis; 31 (l)©Gianni Dagli/Corbis, (cl)©Francis G. Mayer/Corbis, (cr)Album/Oronoz/Newscom, (r)DEA PICTURE LIBRARY/De Agostini Picture Library/Getty Images; 41 (t)altrendo images/Altrendo/Getty Images; 42-43 ©Paul Conklin/Photo Edit Inc.; 43 (t)©K.M. Westermann/Corbis, (r)©Kit Houghton/Corbis; 50 (t)©Stocktrek/Getty Images, (b)©Nathan Bilow/Allsport/Getty Images; 54 (t)©Craig Lovell/Corbis, (b) Gavin Hellier/Robert Harding World Imagery/Getty Images; 57 (b)Rhienna Cutler/E+/Getty Images; 61 (l)Popperfoto/Getty Images, (r)©Niday Picture Library/Alamy; 62-63 Christopher Futcher/Getty Images; 63 (t)©iStockphoto.com/Lya_Cattel, (b)Kristin Piljay/Lonely Planet Images/Getty Images; 67 ©Hero/Corbis/Glow Images; 72 © Bob Krist/Corbis; 76 Fuse/Getty Images; 80 James Balog/age fotostock; 82 Photodisc/Getty Images; 83 (t)© Ken Reid/The Image Bank/Getty Images, (b)©Getty Images; 84-85 Africa Mayi/Moment Open/Getty Images; 85 (t)©Jeremy Horner/Corbis, (b)©Rolf Brenner/Alamy; 99 (t)Getty Images/iStockphoto, (b)GARDEL Bertrand/hemis.fr/Getty Images; 102 Lew Robertson/Photolibrary/Getty Images; 103 Visual Communications/iStock/Getty Images; 104-105 Chandra Dhas/iStock/Getty Images; 105 (t)©Massimo Listri/Corbis, (b)Mel Yates/The Image Bank/Getty Images; 123 (t)©Bettmann/Corbis, (b)©Corbis; 124-125 ©Richard Glover/Corbis; 125 (inset)©Danny Lehman/Corbis; 128 (tl)boggy22/iStock/Getty Images, (tc bl bc)©Richard Glover/Corbis; 131 vertraut/iStock/Getty Images; 133 ©Jose Carillo/Photo Edit Inc.; 142 (l)Cusp/SuperStock, (c)©Corbis, (r)Ariel Skelley/Blend Images/Getty Images; 145 ©Paul Almasy/Corbis; 146-147 ©Pablo Corral V/Corbis; 147 (t)ERproductions Ltd/Blend Images/Getty Images, (b)©Massimo Listri/Corbis; 159 JGI/Blend Images/Getty Images; 165 (t)© AngeloHornak/Corbis, (b)©Terry Whittaker/Frank Lane Picture Agency/Corbis; 166-167 ©L. Clarke/Corbis; 167 ©Y.Levy/Alamy; 169 Cultura Travel/UBACH/DE LA RIVA/Getty Images; 174 Leslie Harris/Photolibrary/Getty Images; 178 ©Getty Images; 179 (l)Isy Ochoa/SuperStock/Getty Images, (r)Yale University Art Gallery; 187 ©Jeremy Horner/Corbis; 188-189 Rawdon Wyatt/Alamy; 189 (t)Kathrin Ziegler/Taxi/Getty Images, (b)Daniel Korzeniewski/Hemera/Getty Images; 192 Lew Robertson/Photolibrary/Getty Images; 204 McGraw-Hill Education; 209 ©Hubert Stadler/Corbis; 210-211 ©Michelle Garrett/Corbis; 211 (t)© Owen Franken/Corbis, (r)Alberto Rojas Serrano/Moment/Getty Images; 223 Scott Bauer/USDA; 230 DEA/G. DAGLI ORTI/De Agostini/Getty Images; 231 ©Marc Serota/Rueters Newmedia Inc/Corbis; 232-233 ©Hello World Stock Library /Alamy; 233 (t)Tetra Images/Alamy, (b)©R H Productions/Robert Harding World Imagery/Corbis; 239 (l)©Christie's Images/Corbis, (r)©Leemage/Corbis; 253 (t)©Christie's Images/Corbis; 254-255 Lauree Feldman/Photolibrary/Getty Images; 255 (r)John Elk/Lonely Planet Images/Getty Images; 275 (t)Arlene Richie/Media Sources/The LIFE Images Collection/Getty Images, (b)John Parra/Getty Images Entertainment/Getty Images.